SIDS

*A Parent's Guide to
Understanding and Preventing
Sudden Infant Death
Syndrome*

Also by William Sears, M.D.

The Discipline Book
The Birth Book
The Baby Book
300 Questions New Parents Ask
The Fussy Baby
Nighttime Parenting
Creative Parenting
Becoming a Father

SIDS

A Parent's Guide to

Understanding and Preventing

Sudden Infant Death

Syndrome

WILLIAM SEARS, M.D.

LITTLE, BROWN AND COMPANY

Boston   New York   Toronto   London

Copyright © 1995 by William Sears

First Edition

"Could You Please Just Listen?" by Debbie Gemmill. Copyright ©
by Debbie Gemmill. By permission of the author.

Library of Congress Cataloging-in-Publication Data

Sears, William, M.D.
    SIDS : a parent's guide to understanding and preventing Sudden Infant Death
Syndrome / William Sears. — 1st ed.
        p.   cm.
    Includes bibliographical references and index.
    ISBN 0-316-77912-1
    1. Sudden infant death syndrome.   I. Title.
RJ320.S93S43   1995
618.92 — dc20   95-7045

10 9 8 7 6 5 4 3 2 1

MV-NY

Drawings by Deborah Maze

Published simultaneously in Canada by Little, Brown & Company (Canada) Limited

Printed in the United States of America

Contents

Many Thanks

This book would not have been written without the help and encouragement of so many contributors. First, my thanks go to the hundreds of concerned parents who shared with me their worry about SIDS and repeatedly asked me, "Is there anything we can do to prevent this tragedy from happening in our family?" Thanks also to SIDS researchers Eric Gibson, M.D., W. Brendle Glomb, M.D., and Thomas Keens, M.D., for their critical review of the scientific validity of this book. A heartfelt thanks to the many SIDS parents who critiqued this manuscript and offered useful suggestions; I especially thank Jill and John Lazzarini, Cheri Purcell, Debbie Gemmill, Joani Nelson Horchler, and Leigh Julius.

Thanks to the many wise parents who read the manuscript and guided me toward the best way to help other parents reduce their worry and reduce the risk, especially, Gwen Gotsch, Kathy Nesper, Jan Whitcomb, Kelly Brennan, and Stacy Prince. Much gratitude goes to my research assistants, Nancy Samp and Ivana Jeric. Thanks also to my assistant Tracee Zeni for her dedication to word processing. A special thanks goes to bereavement counselor Georgiana Rodiger, Ph.D., for her review of the "Healthy Grieving" chapter. I wish to thank editor Jennifer Josephy and copyeditor Pamela Marshall at Little, Brown for their patience and guidance through the many rewrites leading up to the finished manuscript. Finally, unending praise goes to the SIDS Alliance organization and their nationwide SIDS support groups, many of whose members shared with me the most common worries new parents have and helped me to stay focused on the goal of this book: to reduce the risk of SIDS.

A Word from Dr. Bill

Each year six thousand babies in the United States go to sleep and never wake up. No one knows why. Even though Sudden Infant Death Syndrome (SIDS) is one of the least likely tragedies that could happen in a family, it is one of the highest on parents' worry lists. I have written this book in the belief that parents who are informed more worry less. Throughout *A Parent's Guide to Understanding and Preventing SIDS,* I present information to reduce your worry and practical ways to reduce the risk. One of my goals in writing this book is to take some of the mystery out of SIDS by exposing the myth that there is little parents can do and by offering practical risk-reduction methods that rely on a combination of good science and plain common sense. While the program suggested in this book is no guarantee, it will drastically reduce the chance of SIDS occurring in your family.

Some steps in the proposed SIDS risk-reduction program are supported by research; other steps are hypothetical. Yet nothing in this book is sheer speculation. Throughout this book I have referenced those parts of the risk-reduction program that are supported by research and indicated those that are not. You will notice that whenever I propose a way of reducing the risk of SIDS that is not scientifically proven, I take you through the reasoning process that led me to this conclusion.

I want you to enjoy your baby. Most babies are healthy and stay that way. Don't let the fear of SIDS ruin this enjoyment. Take as much of the risk-lowering advice as fits your family and then sit back and enjoy your life together.

William Sears, M.D.
San Clemente, Calif.
June 1995

I

Understanding SIDS

Parents need a basic knowledge about the physiological principles of how babies breathe and sleep; by understanding these principles, parents will have a better handle on how parenting practices can make a difference in how their babies sleep and breathe. Until the past decade, Sudden Infant Death Syndrome (SIDS) was a mystery without a solution, a tragedy without a prevention. While SIDS still remains somewhat of a puzzle, new research has shed some light on its cause and, even more encouraging, its prevention. This part of the book deals with the latest SIDS research, especially that which pertains to lowering the risk of SIDS.

The term "prevention" is used throughout this book to mean *reducing the risk* of SIDS, in the same way as a healthy diet is called "preventive" medicine for heart disease even though it is not a guarantee against heart attacks.

1

How This Book Evolved

It's the call every pediatrician dreads. It came at three o'clock on a cold morning in the winter of 1972. I picked up the receiver and heard a mother's voice on the other end: "Doctor, my baby's dead!" Incredulous, I rushed over to her home and found devastated parents holding their lifeless baby. The paramedics had just left. I will never forget the look of shock and disbelief on the faces of the parents. That was the first time I witnessed the grief and shock caused by Sudden Infant Death Syndrome (SIDS).

I've never felt so helpless. "Doctor, why did this happen?" the mother asked me. "My baby had her three-month checkup just a week ago, and she was so healthy. Five hours ago she was nursing contentedly. Now she's dead. What happened?" The parents groped for answers, and I had none.

A few days later I again sat with these parents as they begged for answers that nobody could give them. "What did the autopsy show?" they probed. "Nothing," I answered feebly. "So you don't know why our baby died?" they persisted. "No, I don't." "Can we prevent this from happening again if we have another baby? Is there anything we can do?" All I could muster was a faint "I don't know." But to look parents in the eye and tell them there's nothing that can be done to lower their chances of losing another baby to SIDS went against my beliefs and my training. My years as a medical student taught me that there are scientific answers to most things. It's just a matter of finding them. As I sat helplessly in front of these parents I hoped that someday I would be able to look confidently into the eyes of other parents and say, "Yes, here is what you can do to lessen your chances of your baby dying of SIDS." This book is a fulfillment of that hope.

My initial experience with SIDS turned me into a student of the syndrome, which is defined as *the sudden death of an infant under one year of age that remains unexplained.* Over the next ten years, I read the research, attended scientific meetings, and tried to glean clues to this grim mystery from every possible source. Even though the general opinion of researchers echoed the then-official position of the American Academy of Pediatrics — that SIDS could not be predicted or prevented — I did not believe it. And, in the 1970s and early 1980s, I found that there was a lot of valuable information about SIDS in existence, though it stayed in research laboratories or lay buried in obscure medical journals and was never shared with parents.

I also learned a lot by listening to parents. One piece of advice I offer to pediatricians about to enter practice is "Surround yourself with wise parents — and learn from them." I became a keen parent-and-baby-watcher. Every time a mother or father shared something with me about their parenting style that I thought could affect the general health of a baby and even remotely influence the risk of SIDS, I filed this bit of wisdom. (See pages 126–134 for examples of what parents shared with me.) By the early eighties my files were bulging, but I was no further along in solving this mystery than any of the other equally frustrated students of SIDS. I was still largely unable to answer the question "What can we do to prevent our baby from dying of SIDS?" I had lots of disorganized information but no practical advice. It was time for a new approach.

I decided to start with a working hypothesis of what causes

SIDS and to use this, along with the available research, to speculate about what could be done to prevent this tragedy. My hypothesis would be nothing more than an educated hunch — based on research and a bit of common sense. At least it was a starting point. There are holes in many of the current SIDS hypotheses, including mine. That's because SIDS is not quite as simple as "Here is what it is, and this is what you can do about it."

I started with the two basic facts about SIDS that intrigued me the most. First, *babies stop breathing and die in their sleep.* From this I reasoned, as have other researchers, that SIDS (at least in most infants) must be a *disorder of breathing during sleep.* Normally, breathing starts and stops automatically, even during sleep. Could something occur during sleep that prevents babies from automatically starting to breathe again after a long pause? Are some infants more likely than others to stop breathing during sleep? Could parents do something to make their babies' automatic breathing mechanisms fail-safe?

The second fact about SIDS that I found interesting was that it nearly always occurs when the baby is between one and six months of age, with a *peak incidence at two to four months.* Why is an infant so vulnerable during this particular stage of development? If we could answer that question, we might be able to take the next logical step and figure out what parents and doctors could do to help babies sleep and breathe safely during this vulnerable time. (What happens during this vulnerable period to make an infant physiologically at risk of SIDS is discussed in the next chapter.)

With these starting points, I formed a hypothesis that was published in 1985 in my book *Nighttime Parenting:*[194] "In those infants at risk for SIDS, natural mothering (unrestricted breastfeeding and sharing sleep with baby) will lower the risk of SIDS." As you will see in Chapters 7 and 8, new research is beginning to validate my original hypothesis.

A MESSAGE TO SIDS RESEARCHERS

Throughout this book I have attempted to be scientifically correct; yet because the field of SIDS research is characterized by conflicting and confusing data, it has sometimes been difficult to glean from the voluminous scientific literature the most credible research — and even more challenging to translate these results into a useful SIDS risk-reduction program for worried parents. Some suggestions in this book are supported by science and others are hypothetical. If my suggestions that are supported only by "common sense" and anecdotal stories offend the scientist in you, consider the fact that despite more than twenty years and millions of dollars spent on SIDS research, SIDS rates have fallen only slightly in the United States. The idea that parenting practices may affect SIDS rates is, admittedly, a departure from traditional thinking about SIDS. But perhaps it is time for a fresh approach to reducing the risk of SIDS.

I believe that "common sense" and "anecdotal" evidence are useful, despite the fact that they are "unscientific." The term "prevention" mentioned throughout this book may raise the eyebrows of purists who use this term to imply total elimination of a problem. I use the term in the same way as a healthy diet can be dubbed "preventive" medicine for heart disease yet not be a guarantee against heart attacks. By "preventive" I mean *practical things a person can do to lower the chances* of this malady happening. Rather than being a comprehensive, scientific review of the field of SIDS, this book is meant to be a useful guide primarily for parents who ask how they can reduce the risk of SIDS happening in their family, and secondly for professionals who offer preventive medical advice.

At the time I emphasized that this was my own hypothesis, based only upon pediatrician's intuition and not upon scientific studies. I formed this hypothesis because I believed it. I published it because I wanted to stimulate SIDS research in the area of prevention. The prevailing opinion was that nighttime parenting practices had no effect on this mysterious malady. I dared to be the first physician to challenge this belief.

Shortly after *Nighttime Parenting* appeared, I received a call from a worried mother who had read the book. Her baby had stop-breathing episodes (apnea) during sleep. She wanted to know what she could do to decrease these episodes. I suggested that this mother take her baby out of the crib and sleep next to her in her bed, offering unrestricted night nursing. After a few nights of this arrangement the mother reported, "It worked!" She was thrilled, and so was I. Yet because of my medical training, I was programmed to be skeptical. I was very aware that my enthusiasm and desire for an answer could cloud my objectivity. Was this purely a coincidence? I asked the mother to put her baby back in the crib for the next three nights along with an electronic infant monitor. Each night the apnea alarm sounded many times. Thereafter, the mother took the baby back into her bed and there were no more alarms. Baby E.Z. never used the crib again.

I was hopeful that we had found a way of reducing the risk of SIDS in infants with a history of apnea, yet I realized that complex problems don't have easy answers. So, although the initials of this baby were E.Z., and privately the parents and I referred to this SIDS-prevention method as the "E.Z. approach," I was cautious. (The story of this baby and the accompanying sleep-sharing precautions are fully discussed on pages 122–124.)

Later that same year I was invited to share my hypothesis and the case of Baby E.Z. with the scientific community at the International Congress of Pediatrics in Honolulu.[195] My presentation received mixed reviews. Pediatricians from other parts of the world were accepting and said my approach "made sense" and warranted further study. Pediatricians in the United States were skeptical: "It's too simple."

While I was researching my hypothesis within my pediatric practice, I wrote about it frequently, hoping to encourage academics to study the effect of different nighttime parenting styles on infant breathing. There are many serious scientists in university laboratories who derive their fame and fortune from research, so I was confident that sooner or later this obvious void in the SIDS literature would be filled. Between 1985 and 1993, I carefully followed SIDS research, collected valuable information from parents, and undertook studies on one of our own babies (which I will elaborate on later, page 120).

The experts — parents who have lost a baby to SIDS — gave me the focus for my work. I hung around SIDS parents at SIDS conferences trying to glean from grieving parents their most pressing needs. Needless to say, their perspective was very different from that of the researchers, who know SIDS from the laboratory but who have never experienced the personal tragedy of finding their baby dead. In a way I felt like an outsider in a club that I certainly didn't want to be a member of. Yet I learned the three questions parents most wanted answers to: Why SIDS? Why us? What can we do to prevent it from happening again? These questions became the basis for this book.

In 1993 my wife, Martha, and I put all of our information together for the first time in a section on SIDS prevention in *The Baby Book*.[197] We listed practical steps parents could take to lower the risk of SIDS. The response from professionals and parents to our proposed SIDS prevention program was gratifying. Most professionals agreed with us, although some were wary, claiming that some of our conclusions were not scientifically proven. They were right, and we were quick to agree that we could not claim that if parents practiced these suggestions their baby would definitely not die of SIDS. Yet we remain confident that this program lowers the risk. Many of the parents who read *The Baby Book* have told us how thankful they were to find something they could do to ease their worries about SIDS. Because of this response, I decided to expand and update this SIDS prevention program into *A Parent's Guide to Understanding and Preventing SIDS*. As you will see, each part of our SIDS prevention method is referenced to scientific studies from the medical literature. To these I have added some preliminary research of my own, plus a pinch of common sense.

When we first proposed the SIDS prevention program in *The Baby Book*, Martha and I feared we might needlessly worry parents. After all, 99.8 percent of babies don't die of SIDS. Yet we discovered our fear was unfounded. Parents told us that being better informed about how they could reduce the risk of SIDS lessened their worry. When they discovered that there were practical things they could do to prevent SIDS, they felt less helpless and more in control of the situation.

Initially, I intended this book for one group of readers: new parents who ask the question "What can we do to lower the risk of SIDS happening to our baby?" Yet I realized that parents who had lost their baby to SIDS groped for answers, and they would also read this book. I faced a dilemma of informing new parents about how to keep their babies alive without instilling guilt in parents whose babies had died. I worried that SIDS parents would feel that if they had taken all these preventive measures their baby might be alive today. My worry was unwarranted. When I shared my dilemma with SIDS parents, they told me that after the initial grieving period they became more interested in the future than the past, and they eagerly embraced any informa-

A MESSAGE TO SIDS PARENTS

I wrote this book primarily for new parents who say, "I worry so much about SIDS. Is there anything I can do to prevent it?" However, I realize that SIDS parents (those parents who have lost a child to SIDS, and who have already suffered more than anyone should) in their unending search for answers, will also read it, and some of the new information contained in this book may trigger uncomfortable feelings, such as guilt ("If only I had done these things") or anger ("Why didn't someone inform me?"). Please try to keep in mind the audience for whom this book is written and my goal in writing it, to lower the rate of SIDS. In presenting a seven-step SIDS risk-reduction program, in no way am I implying that *all* SIDS cases can be predicted or prevented — neither now nor when your baby died. Also, I am not implying that SIDS parents were not vigilant or nurturing enough to keep their babies alive.

As a parent of eight, I am painfully aware that nothing could be more devastating than the death of a child, and nothing could be more heart-piercing than the guilt feelings that in some way you might have prevented it. Please take consolation in the knowledge that you did the best you could, given the prevailing parenting advice at the time. It was not your fault your baby died, and even if you had taken all the seven steps of the risk-reduction program in this book, your baby still might have died.

Also, because of the widespread statistics circulated about SIDS risk reduction, I worry that parents may get the message that "the typical" SIDS mother takes drugs, smokes, feeds her baby artificial baby milk, and engages in unsafe sleeping habits. This portrayal is untrue and unfair. Many SIDS babies die despite having a healthy womb environment, being breastfed, enjoying safe sleeping habits and a nurturing home, and so on. If you read a passage in this book that sets off disturbing feelings, please remember my main purpose in writing this book. I have attempted to put together a useful guide to parents that, while admittedly no SIDS-free guarantee, will, I believe, reduce the risk of this tragedy in the future.

tion that might uncover answers to this grim mystery. They felt that being informed about SIDS prevention could keep this from happening to another of their babies, or to babies of friends. As one mother told me, "Nothing could make me feel worse than I do already. I need answers."

To SIDS parents who read the seven-step risk-reduction program and feel "If only I had . . . ," please remember that the program proposed in this book is not a SIDS-free guarantee. Also, remember that when you lost an infant to SIDS, you were doing everything you could do, given the advice and baby-care customs of the times. Parents blaming themselves for the death of a baby from SIDS when the information on lowering the risk was not available to them is somewhat akin to parents blaming themselves for their child's death from pneumonia before the discovery of penicillin.

Even though SIDS is a relatively rare tragedy, it is still the primary cause of death in infants between one month and one year, and as a pediatrician I can testify that it is the number one worry of new parents. For that reason, I have researched and reported to the best of my ability the latest and most credible research on the subject, to help you be prepared, but not paranoid, about SIDS.

This is not a wimpy book. It is meant to be read by parents who have serious worries about SIDS and who want an answer to the question "Is there anything we can do to lower the risk of this happening to our baby?" Because of the nature of this topic, I realize that by talking about it I risk pushing sensitive buttons. This is unavoidable. Unless I speak frankly, this book will be nothing more than a watered-down version of the real story, with a lot of "I don't knows" and "there's nothing you can dos."

I've tried to take the puzzle of SIDS apart piece by piece, examine each piece in detail, and then put the pieces back together into a workable program that any parent can understand and use. I would ask that you approach each part of the SIDS prevention program with an open mind, analyzing the scientific basis for my conclusions and, even more important, running it through your own internal sensor. Ask yourself: Does this seem to be a suggestion that makes sense for our family? I assure you that each statement I make has been well researched and critiqued by credible colleagues. Because much of the information is bound to lift the eyebrows of skeptics, I have referenced controversial statements in case readers want to verify my conclusions.

Because SIDS is a sensitive topic, some physicians and researchers may feel compelled to question all or part of my proposed SIDS prevention program. I welcome these questions and hope that they will stimulate further research. In addition to lacking sufficient financial support, current SIDS research lacks direction. One of my purposes in writing this book is to help steer SIDS research in the direction of prevention, especially in relation to the effect of various parenting styles on SIDS risk.

Whether or not this SIDS prevention program works will be

answered only by the test of time, but I am certain that whatever the effects on SIDS rates, this program will make babies physically and psychologically healthier, and will strengthen the parent-child connection. All the steps in this risk-reduction program are plain and simple good parenting — and safe parenting.

2

SIDS Basics: Why SIDS?
Why *My* Baby?

Two questions parents invariably have about SIDS are what causes it and what can they do to prevent it? Because of the nature of this mystery, complete answers to those questions are unavailable, yet there is much new research on which infants are most at risk of SIDS and what parents can do to lower that risk.

QUESTIONS ABOUT SIDS

The following are the questions parents most often ask about SIDS.

What is SIDS?

Sudden Infant Death Syndrome is the sudden death of an infant under one year of age that remains unexplained after the performance of a complete postmortem investigation, including an autopsy, an examination of the scene of death, and a review of the case history.[242] This is the 1991 international definition agreed upon by SIDS researchers, who believe it is important to have a uniform definition of SIDS in order to collect meaningful information that would apply to SIDS prevention from country to country.

How often does SIDS occur?

SIDS is the leading cause of death in infants between one month and one year of age, accounting for approximately 40 percent of infant deaths in the United States. In the United States it occurs in approximately 1 in 700 babies. (SIDS incidence is customarily expressed in deaths per one thousand infants. The incidence in the United States as of 1994 was *1.3 to 1.5 per thousand,* a decrease from 1.7 per thousand in 1984.[37, 242a]) The incidence varies around the world from one-tenth of the U.S. figure to five times this number, depending on the definition of SIDS and how it is reported and investigated in various countries. Around six thousand babies die in the United States from SIDS each year.

When is SIDS most likely to occur?

Ninety percent of SIDS cases occur *by six months* of age. Most SIDS cases occur between two and four months of age, with the peak incidence around three months of age. SIDS does occur, but is uncommon, below the age of one month and past the age of six months. SIDS occurs during an infant's sleep, either nighttime or naptime. Most SIDS infants are discovered between 10:00 P.M. and 10:00 A.M., the usual hours of prolonged infant sleep. The peak time of death seems to be around 5:00 A.M.[60] SIDS is more likely to occur on weekends and holidays, and there are several possible explanations for this curious statistic: For example, this could be a time of less access to medical care or a period when there are more likely to be changes in care-giving practices.

SIDS is more common during cold-weather months.[104] In the Northern Hemisphere, the January SIDS rate is double the July rate. In the Southern Hemisphere, the incidence of SIDS during July is nearly double that during January. There are two plausible explanations for the increased cold-weather risk of SIDS: respiratory infections are more common during cold months, and sleeping conditions may be more risky for some babies, specifically an overheated bedroom or overwrapping. (See discussion of overheating as a risk factor of SIDS in Chapter 9.)

These are the two most intriguing factors about SIDS:

- SIDS occurs during an infant's sleep.
- SIDS is most common from two to four months of age.

Much of my approach to why SIDS occurs and what can be done to lower the risk is based on an understanding of how special developmental features that appear around this age may contribute to SIDS risk. Parents can help their baby through this vulnerable age by being aware of these factors and by taking steps to lower the risk. (See "The Developmental Dip," page 34.)

Is SIDS more common in boys or girls? Does it happen more often in some cultures than in others?

For unknown reasons, SIDS is higher in males than in females by a ratio of 1.5 to 1. Infant mortality for most diseases is slightly higher in males. The increased incidence of SIDS in some races (for example, SIDS occurs more often among African Americans than among Caucasians) is thought to be more likely the result of differences in childcare practices, education, and socioeconomics than race itself, yet even when correcting for these factors, African American families have a higher incidence of SIDS. Some cultures have a particularly high incidence of SIDS (for example, Native Americans and Aborigines in other countries, such as New Zealand). SIDS is lower among Hispanics and even lower in Asian cultures. Some of the differences in SIDS rates may be due to cultural differences in risk factors, such as smoking, safe sleeping arrangements, and type of healthcare. These and other risk factors will be discussed throughout this book.

IMMUNIZATIONS AND SIDS — NO CORRELATION

Immunizations do not cause SIDS. Statements implicating immunizations as causing SIDS are unproven and false, causing parents to worry needlessly, and perhaps depriving of proper immunization some infants whose parents want to give them the safest medical care. The reason for this unfortunate bad press is coincidental: The peak period of SIDS (two to four months) occurs at the same time that most babies get their shots, so that SIDS rates would be expected to be higher at the same time immunization rates are. This is an example of the fallacy of correlation implying causation. One of the infants in my practice died of SIDS the morning he was to have his two-month well-baby checkup and his first shot. Had this baby died only a few hours later, after the immunization, the shot would have been unfairly blamed.

Several large studies have shown no cause and effect between immunization and SIDS.[78, 96, 97, 183] In fact, statistically, lack of routine immunizations carries a higher risk of SIDS. SIDS rates increase during pertussis (whooping cough) outbreaks. A recent study even showed a drop in SIDS rates following the routine use of the HIB vaccine. These findings of higher SIDS rates in underimmunized infants may reflect the high risk of SIDS in infants who receive less routine medical care.

Are some babies more at risk of SIDS than others?

Yes. While many babies dying of SIDS have no previous warning signs or apparent risk factors, some infants are at higher risk than others. The term "risk factor" refers to some element in the baby's environment or development that increases the chances of dying

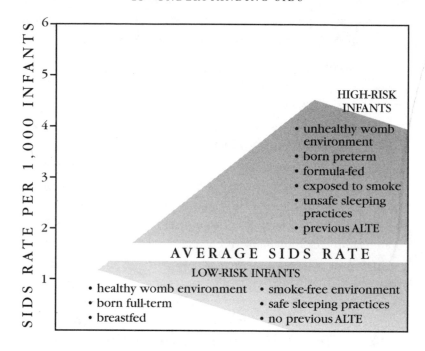

of SIDS. It is a clue, something associated with SIDS, not a cause. "Risk factor" means only that there is a statistical increase in SIDS among the overall population of babies who have that factor. It is not a death sentence for an individual infant. For example, infants whose mothers smoke pre- or postnatally have a higher risk of dying of SIDS than babies of mothers who do not smoke. But this does not mean that SIDS is common among children of smokers. Though more babies of smokers than babies of nonsmokers will die of SIDS, most babies of smokers will not die of SIDS. A batter with one strike against him has an increased risk of striking out; a batter with two strikes, even more. But the increased risk doesn't necessarily mean he will strike out. Identifying risk factors is important; if you know what increases the risk of SIDS, you know what you can do to lower it.

Infants at higher risk of SIDS include the following:

- premature infants
- infants whose mothers smoked or took illegal drugs during pregnancy
- infants whose parents smoke around them after birth
- infants who are put down to sleep on their stomachs
- infants who are not breastfed
- infants who have had an ALTE (apparent life-threatening event), such as a stop-breathing episode in which the baby was pale, blue, and limp (the older term for this was "near-miss SIDS")
- infants of mothers with little or no prenatal care and those from a poor socioeconomic environment
- siblings of a previous SIDS baby (only a slightly increased risk; see page 207 for explanation)

Please note that most infants having these risk factors don't die of SIDS, and some infants dying of SIDS don't have any of these risk factors. Even babies with *all* of these risk factors have a *less than 1 percent* chance of dying of SIDS.

If neither my baby nor my family has any of these risk factors, what are my baby's chances of dying of SIDS?

Even "pure" babies (those without any of the risk factors) die of SIDS, but their death rate is much lower. SIDS authorities believe the rate of SIDS is reduced by 50 percent if none of these risk factors are present. Mathematically, that translates into a rate reduction from 1 in 700 to 1 in 1,400. The good news is that most of the known risk factors are under a parent's control.

Are SIDS babies different from other infants?

This is a question that divides SIDS researchers and confuses SIDS readers. Like many questions in child health, there are few areas

WHAT DOES "HIGH RISK" MEAN?

Throughout this book you will see the term "high-risk SIDS baby." Like the term "high-risk pregnancy," this sounds scary, and if not properly understood it can cause needless anxiety. Certain groups of infants have higher chances of succumbing to SIDS than others. The two highest-risk groups are infants who have experienced an ALTE and infants who are born prematurely. Other babies at high risk are infants of drug-addicted mothers and infants of mothers who smoked during pregnancy. But keep in mind that "high risk" is only a *statistical* term, and does not imply that *your* infant may die of SIDS, even if he or she has these risk factors. Even though high-risk infants may have a "ten times greater chance of SIDS," realistically, that translates into a risk of around one in fifty chances. And while your baby may have a higher statistical risk of SIDS, there may be things you as a parent can do to lower this risk.

of black and white but many shades of gray. The question merits a "no and yes" answer. No — it seems that most infants dying of SIDS are not developmentally different from other infants. But yes — *some* infants dying of SIDS *are* developmentally different. (These differences are discussed on page 41.) It may be that if these developmental risk factors are detected soon after birth, parents and professionals can intervene to lower the risk of SIDS in these babies. However, before we delve into how some babies are different, it helps to have an understanding of the complexities of SIDS research and why SIDS remains a syndrome without a clear cause.

SIDS RESEARCH: HOW IS IT DONE?
WHAT'S KNOWN? WHAT'S NEW?

There are many ways to study the frightening mystery of SIDS. One is the *epidemiological,* or *statistical, approach.* By gathering information on a large number of SIDS infants over a long period of time and looking for patterns and similarities, it is possible to identify factors that occur more often in SIDS infants than in non-SIDS infants. This statistical approach is how the risk factors listed on page 19 were identified. The epidemiological approach gives a *general* view of the problem, but it suffers from the usual problem with statistics: The results may or may not apply to an individual baby. Yet, the epidemiological approach is at least a starting point for uncovering clues to the mystery. If a certain factor, for example, maternal smoking, occurs more frequently in SIDS infants, the next question to ask is how exactly does smoke harm a baby's ability to breathe during sleep? The statistical approach guides investigators toward asking the right questions, even though finding the right answers continues to frustrate researchers and parents.

Another problem with the large statistical studies is that they are mostly *retrospective.* Parents are interviewed and death scene circumstances are investigated *after the fact,* when parents' recall may be fuzzy or distorted by their reaction to their child's death. (After losing a baby, some parents can give an incredibly accurate account of their baby's medical history, and even the circumstances preceding the death; others can't.)

Another avenue of research is the *physiological* approach. Is there something different in the brain, heart, lungs, or other system of SIDS babies? If researchers could answer this question, it is possible a remedy could be found. For example, high cholesterol levels in adults signal a higher risk of a heart attack; adults with high cholesterol can lower their risks by making changes in their lifestyle and diet, and by taking medication. The problem in SIDS research, of course, is how to study hearts and lungs that are no longer pumping and breathing. One possible alternative is to study a baby who almost died — a sort of SIDS survivor, a baby who survived an apparently life-threatening event (ALTE). Researchers also study infants with many of the risk factors for SIDS to determine if their breathing control mechanisms work any differently than those of "normal" infants. Are these "at risk" infants physiologically different? Like other avenues of SIDS research, this area of study yields "yes," "no," and "maybe" results.

For example, studies on infants at risk of SIDS have shown that many of these infants have diminished arousability from sleep in response to breathing problems.[102, 109] In other words, these infants seem to have a less reliable respiratory control center. A clue? Maybe. Along comes another study that calls this one into question. It seems that some "normal" or "low-risk" infants also show this same "abnormality" of diminished arousability; when infant apnea monitoring was first used it detected stop-breathing episodes in infants at risk, but further studies revealed that low–risk infants also have apnea episodes. This phenomenon, which plagues SIDS researchers, is called "overlap" — the same "abnormalities" that occur in high-risk infants also occur in some low-risk infants. These discoveries make it difficult to interpret "abnormal" findings because we still don't have a clear appreciation of what is "normal" breathing in babies. To date, other than the risk factors listed on page 19, there are no known physiological predictors of SIDS reliable enough to merit tagging an individual baby.

Another way of trying to solve the puzzle of SIDS is through postmortem examination of SIDS infants. Because no cause of death is found on autopsy, SIDS is often called a diagnosis of exclusion. The examiner knows what didn't happen, but can't determine what did. This does not mean the answer is unknowable.

It may mean that the examiner has neither the knowledge nor the means to identify what went wrong. Expertise in SIDS knowledge varies among pathologists, as do the resources available to perform comprehensive postmortem examinations.

While some pathologists believe there are no distinguishing postmortem characteristics ("markers") of SIDS babies, others believe it depends upon how hard pathologists look for clues. Early postmortem research on SIDS babies revealed changes in the blood vessels of the lungs and other organs that suggested the infant may have been experiencing chronic oxygen deprivation.[164, 165] Other investigators have found injury to the cells near the respiratory control center in the brain.[116] In their quest to solve the mystery of SIDS, pathologists have left no tissue untested. One study, yet to be replicated, showed that SIDS infants had larger tongues than babies dying of other causes — a factor that could obstruct breathing.[203] Autopsies on some SIDS babies revealed pinpoint hemorrhages (called "intrathoracic petechiae") in the chest organs, namely the heart and lungs.[126, 127] These hemorrhages probably occurred during a breathing obstruction; the negative pressure in the chest increases in order to get air in, and the force is great enough to break blood vessels. (You may have experienced a similar phenomenon yourself if you have ever popped a blood vessel in your face when pushing in childbirth or blowing or coughing hard.) These are promising clues, but still they are only clues.

To achieve credibility, any scientific breakthrough must be *replicated,* that is, other researchers must be able to duplicate the study. The more times researchers come to the same conclusion, the more likely it is the discovery is true. Some of these postmortem findings have failed this test. Whether it's because of differences in methods from one researcher to another or because the conclusions were not really valid in the first place remains an unanswered question. However, it seems that the postmortem studies showing abnormalities in the brain tissues that affect respiratory control are surviving the rigors of replication.

Sometimes trying to be "scientific" hinders SIDS prevention advice. For example, whether breastfeeding lowers SIDS risk is still not agreed upon by many researchers. As I will explain in Chapter 7, the preventive effect of breastfeeding on SIDS is unlikely ever to be proven by blind, replicated, controlled studies.* Not only are there too many other variables, but the ethics of requiring a mother not to breastfeed — for the sake of a study — are questionable. In this case, we must rely on pure and simple *common sense*.

The *prospective* approach is another way of studying SIDS: perform physiological studies on thousands of infants while they are living. Then, after some of these babies go on to die of SIDS, analyze the data to see what was different about the babies who died. With SIDS affecting only 1 baby in 700, you can imagine how many thousands of babies would have to be studied in order to come up with enough SIDS cases to yield valid results. Nevertheless, one study like this was done.[204, 205] Researchers performed electrocardiograms on approximately ten thousand infants between one month and six months of age. Twenty-nine of these babies later died of presumed SIDS. Initial analysis showed no statistically significant difference between the electrocardiograms of the babies who lived and the babies who died. A disappointment? Not necessarily. Years later, using improved computerized technology, the data from this study was reanalyzed, and researchers found that the heartbeats of some of the SIDS babies were in fact different from the non-SIDS ba-

---

*"Blind" and "control" are research jargon for the scientific credibility of a study. For example, to make their findings more objective when comparing the tissues of SIDS infants and infants who died of known causes (controls), the examiners are "blind" to which infants they are studying.

bies.[102, 190, 245] Normally, a person's heart rate changes regularly in response to changing physiological demands. The heartbeats of SIDS babies in this study showed less beat-to-beat variability than the heartbeats of infants who lived. Physiologists believe this discovery suggests that SIDS babies may have problems in the way their nervous system controls the heart. Perhaps SIDS infants are less able to adjust their heart rates to changing physiological conditions, and thus their hearts may not pump enough blood to tissues involved in respiratory control. Studies such as these are encouraging, but in this case, because of the problem of overlap (many non-SIDS infants also showed the same heart rate pattern), this finding was not specific enough to justify doing electrocardiograms on every newborn.

When home monitoring entered the SIDS scene, parents and researchers hoped this electronic detector would reveal clues and save lives, and this highly touted technology has done both. Computer records reveal what was happening immediately before a baby's last breath and heartbeat. Some records, however, are confusing, and observers disagree on what they mean.[112] More recent studies, using the newest monitors (see "Infant Home Monitoring: Who and How Long?" page 55), reveal that in some infants who either died or were about to die there were abnormalities in heartbeat *before* any problem occurred in the baby's breathing. Usually SIDS is considered to be primarily a breathing problem and not a heart problem, but this may not always be the case.[111]

Another promising avenue in the search for clues to SIDS is to perform breathing studies (called "pneumograms") on sleeping newborns who are at higher risk of SIDS (premature infants, for example, or newborns who show apnea episodes). Again, the problems of overlap and nonspecificity squelch any possibility of using pneumograms to predict SIDS.[83, 103]

Even with all these studies looking in so many directions for the causes of SIDS, to date there are no screening tests to predict

SIDS AND SUBSTITUTE CARE

In reading the medical literature on the conditions in which babies die, I'm astounded at how many deaths occur while infants are in the care of substitutes. Most cases were due to unsafe sleeping practices and avoidable accidents, such as putting baby to sleep in an unsafe bed.[13, 70]

In other cases, babies died while sleeping in a bed that was strange to them (such as when making the transition from parents' bed to crib or when sleeping away from home). I call this "the strange bed phenomenon." Could these infants already be vulnerable to SIDS and the strange bed be one upset too many to their sleep physiology? Could this upset be due to a panic reaction, an exaggerated separation anxiety in going from the familiar to the unfamiliar? These are among the many mysteries about SIDS that need to be solved.

If your child is cared for by substitutes, such as in a daycare program, make sure the caregivers observe the following SIDS-reduction practices: placing baby on back to sleep; not smoking; avoiding unsafe bedding and overheating; and isolating babies who are sick. In addition, consider providing bottles of your own expressed milk instead of using formula.

Babies can die of SIDS even in the care of nurturing and vigilant substitutes. If your baby died while in the care of someone else, consider the deep guilt that person must endure and the devastating feeling that somehow they failed to uphold their responsibility. A helpful resource for childcare providers who have had a child die while in their care is the booklet "When SIDS Occurs in Childcare Settings," available from the National SIDS Resource Center (see page 211.)

SIDS — no blood tests, X rays, exams, or monitors that can determine if a particular baby has an increased physiological risk of dying of SIDS. Yet hope is on the horizon. Take enough committed investigators supported by enough research money and cheered on by persistent parents and you have the recipe for success. That's what is happening now.

FINALLY, A POSSIBLE BREAKTHROUGH IN SIDS PREVENTION AND RESEARCH

While SIDS research in physiology laboratories has been disappointing, new discoveries from babies' bedrooms are promising. During the six-year period from 1989 to 1994, SIDS research changed directions. Instead of despairing about what is not known about SIDS, researchers have taken what little *is* known and translated these bits of information into suggestions for reducing the risk. The success of these research-based preventive measures is encouraging.

A clue — but not a cure. During the 1980s, as researchers sifted through the enormous volumes of SIDS research then available, a clue emerged. Scientists in Avon, England, had been noticing occasional reports in medical literature suggesting that babies who slept on their backs rather than on their bellies might have a lower chance of succumbing to SIDS. So, in 1989, the Avon Project was launched, headed by Dr. Peter Fleming (who recently confided in me that initially he really didn't believe there was any relationship between SIDS and sleeping position).[60, 61] The emphasis of this campaign was to advise parents not to put their babies to sleep on their stomachs (prone) but rather to put babies to sleep on their backs (supine). The Avon researchers were thrilled by the concurrent *50 percent reduction in SIDS rate* within a year. Soon thereafter, the British government began a national SIDS reduction campaign, which taught four simple messages:

1. Put your baby to sleep on her back or side.
2. Don't smoke around your baby pre- or postnatally.
3. Don't overwrap your baby or overheat your baby's sleeping environment.
4. Seek medical attention early if your baby is not well, and be aware of the fact that your baby may need *less* bedding and clothing rather than more when sick.

The main advice, and the one that got the most publicity, since this simple change was most likely to be followed, was to change baby's sleeping position from belly to back. Five million "Back to Sleep" leaflets were distributed at three different intellectual reading levels. Television campaigns and full-page advertisements in all national newspapers helped spread the safe-sleeping gospel. Telephone help lines were established. Coincidentally, a TV talk show host whose pregnancy the whole country had followed had just lost her baby to SIDS. This widely publicized tragedy further helped kick off the SIDS reduction campaign.

SIDS rates plummet in England. Within three months after the national campaign was launched, surveys showed that nearly 90 percent of mothers were aware of the advice to avoid the front sleeping position. Within a year after the risk-reduction campaign was publicized, there was a 50 percent reduction in the incidence of front-sleeping, and a parallel decline in SIDS rates throughout the United Kingdom. Between the years 1989 and 1993, during the height of the SIDS reduction campaign, the national SIDS rate throughout the United Kingdom had fallen from approximately eighteen hundred babies per year in

1989 to approximately five hundred in 1993 — a 70 percent reduction.[60, 61] As an added perk, there was a decrease in the number of infants dying from *all* causes during this period. (For a discussion of how this campaign influenced mothers' smoking around their babies, see page 74.)

Between 1989 and 1993 the incidence of front-sleeping in Avon (where the SIDS reduction campaign began) fell from 57 percent to less than 1 percent. During that time, the County of Avon went from having the highest SIDS rates to the lowest in the United Kingdom, with SIDS rates falling from 3.2 per thousand in the period of 1985 to 1989 to 0.27 per thousand in 1992. During a fifteen-month period in 1992 and 1993 no infants died of SIDS in Avon.

SIDS rates plummet in other countries. Not only did this national SIDS reduction campaign produce a dramatic decrease in the SIDS rate throughout the United Kingdom, it eliminated the age and seasonal peaks of SIDS. Prior to these intervention programs, nearly every study had shown that the incidence of SIDS peaks in the winter or cold-weather months, and between two and four months of age. Yet the babies dying of SIDS during this intervention program in the United Kingdom did not show these two peaks. Also, the greatest reduction in the number of babies dying of SIDS was among those with no high-risk factors.

One country reducing its SIDS rate by 70 percent — was this a fluke? Read on.

A similar "Back to Sleep" SIDS reduction campaign occurred in New Zealand and Australia, followed by a *50 percent* decrease in national SIDS rates in these two countries. The Netherlands too showed a fascinating change. Prior to 1970, the Netherlands had one of the lowest SIDS rates in the Western world, and Dutch babies slept predominantly on their backs. Then, possibly because of the advice of baby-care professionals, Dutch mothers began putting their babies to sleep on their stomachs. Thereafter, the SIDS rates tripled. After the national Dutch "Back to Sleep" promotion, similar to the one in the United Kingdom, the SIDS rates in the Netherlands fell *40 percent.* Sweden, Denmark, Germany, and Ireland saw a similar decrease in SIDS rates following "Back to Sleep" campaigns in these countries.

Eight countries doing similar risk-reduction campaigns and all getting similar results. This had to be more than coincidence. These findings were a breakthrough in SIDS prevention research. SIDS researchers could finally agree on something. These studies were also a breakthrough in SIDS prevention attitude. Healthcare providers could offer parents practical SIDS reduction advice. Best of all, it was simple enough to follow. These studies finally expanded SIDS research from university laboratories into babies' bedrooms. Now there was something parents could do to reduce the risk of their babies dying of SIDS. They did it; and it worked. Between 1989 and 1992 eight countries had, through public awareness campaigns, influenced parents not to put their babies to sleep prone and had enjoyed a dramatic decrease in the number of babies dying of SIDS.

These sleep-position studies mark a historical turning point in the approach to SIDS prevention. Prior to this discovery, SIDS research had been mired in technicalities. As soon as one researcher discovered a possible way to prevent SIDS, another researcher would disprove the finding. As a result, parents were left with a lot of conflicting research data but nothing that offered any hope for decreasing the chance of their baby dying of SIDS. The changing sleep-position advice finally was something practical that professionals could agree upon and that parents could do.

Americans become believers. Initially, American SIDS researchers were skeptical that front-sleeping contributed to

SIDS. They invoked the scientist's axiom: *correlation doesn't mean causation.* Although scientists could speculate, no one could *prove* how belly-sleeping contributes to SIDS, or why back-sleeping is safer. Furthermore, American authorities rightly believed there must be more to the SIDS mystery than how a baby sleeps. They feared that in the United States, with its mix of cultures and diverse childcare practices, SIDS reduction programs might not work as well as they had in other countries. But American healthcare professionals could no longer ignore the compelling results of SIDS reduction programs in other countries.

So, in April of 1992, the American Academy of Pediatrics cautiously endorsed the back-sleeping position as the preferred way to put babies to sleep. In June of 1994, the U.S. Public Health Service organized a national media blitz to kick off the "Back to Sleep" campaign. There was a national press conference in Washington and major TV coverage, and pamphlets were sent to doctors' offices, healthcare clinics, prenatal education groups, and newborn nurseries. The goal was to distribute four million "Back to Sleep" brochures over a two-year campaign. The demand for these brochures turned out to be greater than the supply and led to one of the largest Government Printing Office projects in the last fifteen years. Low-literacy brochures were printed in English and Spanish. To leave no childcare provider unreached, this media blitz also included the American Association of Retired Persons (AARP), so grandparents could hear the message. Day-care centers were also targeted. The primary message of this campaign was that healthy babies should be placed on their backs or sides to sleep. Included in the "Back to Sleep" pamphlets were secondary messages about breastfeeding, maintaining appropriate heating of baby's bedroom, and using safe bedding. The campaign made available peel-off stickers to be put on cribs to remind babysitters not to put babies to sleep prone. An "800" number was set up: 1-800-505-CRIB.

The national "Back to Sleep" campaign was launched as a joint effort of the U.S. Public Health Service, the American Academy of Pediatrics, the SIDS Alliance, and the Association of SIDS Program Professionals. The "Back to Sleep" brochure can be obtained from: Back to Sleep, P.O. Box 29111, Washington, DC 20040, or call toll-free 1-800-505-CRIB. (A note to healthcare professionals and SIDS resource groups: If you have difficulty reordering this brochure, feel free to make copies of it; all federal government publications are reproducible without permission.)

Even before the initial 1992 American Academy of Pediatrics endorsement of supine-sleeping, during the eight months in 1991 following an article in the *Seattle Times* advising against the use of the prone position for sleeping infants, the incidence of SIDS fell by 52 percent in King County, Washington, where 32 percent of households received the *Seattle Times.* Over the next twelve months, the number of SIDS cases in King County remained at approximately half the previous annual average. At the national level, the April 15, 1992, recommendation of the American Academy of Pediatrics was followed in the next six months by a decrease of 12 percent in the number of SIDS cases compared with the previous year.[206]

It is my hope that this book will help keep SIDS prevention momentum going by convincing parents to embrace these proven risk-lowering factors and perhaps consider others that I believe may also reduce the risk of SIDS.

3

The Pieces, the Puzzle, the Prevention: Putting the Program Together

In developing an approach to lowering the risk of SIDS I first looked at the whole puzzle of SIDS, namely the important facts that are known. Then I analyzed each puzzle piece for its implications in terms of SIDS prevention, namely, how to translate a piece of research information into practical meaning for parents. The seven-step risk-reduction program outlined at the end of this chapter is based on my belief that SIDS is essentially a problem in cardiorespiratory control. Understanding the rationale behind the program will help you better decide how to use the program in your home.

How babies normally breathe, why they sometimes don't, what to do. Deep within everyone's brain lies a master control center, a sort of cellular computer, designed to regulate breathing. It's like a thermostat that turns a furnace on and off when the temperature goes below or above a preset level. This breathing center in the brain (called the "respiratory control center") is preset to maintain a healthy level of oxygen in the blood. When the oxygen level in the blood falls too low or the carbon dioxide level gets too high, such as when a person stops breathing or holds her breath, specialized cells (called "chemoreceptors") strategically located along the major arteries to the brain sense these changes and send a message to the master control center to correct the problem by correcting the breathing. This protective mechanism is supposed to function even when a person is in a deep sleep. Normally this drive to breathe is a fail-safe mechanism that works automatically in babies and adults. Yet in some infants, for some unknown reason, this breathing center does not work automatically. Studies suggest that some infants are born with an immature breathing regulating system.

The ability to arouse from sleep in response to a life-threatening event is a normal protective mechanism present in infants and adults. In some infants this automatic wake-up call mechanism in the brain is defective, putting them at risk for SIDS.

So the most plausible SIDS theory to date is that in most infants SIDS is a *defect in cardiorespiratory control and arousability from sleep.* When their oxygen level falls, their breathing does not automatically restart, nor do they automatically rouse themselves from sleep in response to this life-threatening event. Anything that could help this immature respiratory control center work better, improve the baby's arousability, or provide more of a stimulus to breathing has the potential to save the life of a baby who otherwise might die of SIDS. This is exactly what our SIDS prevention program is designed to do.

THE DEVELOPMENTAL DIP

As discussed, 90 percent of SIDS occur in babies under six months of age, with 60 percent occurring between two and four months. I call this vulnerable period from two to four months of age "the dip." The dip is the most intriguing characteristic of this grim mystery. It must be more than coincidence. What is so ominous about a baby's second to fourth month?

Let's explore the special physiological changes or "shifts" that occur in babies during these early months, and the implications for SIDS.

Babies breathe differently. During the two-to-four-month dip, a shift in breathing physiology occurs. In the first few months, an infant's breathing is governed primarily by lower brain centers, so that breathing is more automatic or by reflex (like acting before you have to think about it). As the infant's brain matures, respiratory control shifts to higher brain centers that are less automatic (like having to think before acting). This is like going from autopilot to manual control of breathing. During this shift, at age two to four months, babies may be more at risk for breathing disturbances. This *vital switch* from reflex to voluntary control of breathing is a crucial transition, and one that is poorly understood. The same protective mechanism that clicks on automatically when needed during the newborn period may not so easily click on during the dip. I suspect a clue to SIDS lies in an understanding of the mechanism involved in this switch.

Furthermore, in the early months, the infant's airway is particularly vulnerable to obstruction. Some infants are known as "obligate nose breathers," meaning, they must have at least one clear nostril to breathe. (By six months, most infants have shifted to nose- *and* mouth-breathing, so that if their noses are stuffed, they automatically change to breathing through their mouths.) Some breathing vulnerabilities during the early months are anatomic: there is less bony support keeping the airway open, and the high position of the larynx in infants makes it more susceptible to blockage should the tongue fall backward. During sleep the muscles keeping open the upper airway relax, reducing the size of the air passage. In time, the larynx descends away from the tongue, and the bony support for the upper airway improves.[23, 221, 222] Babies literally grow out of this anatomical risk.

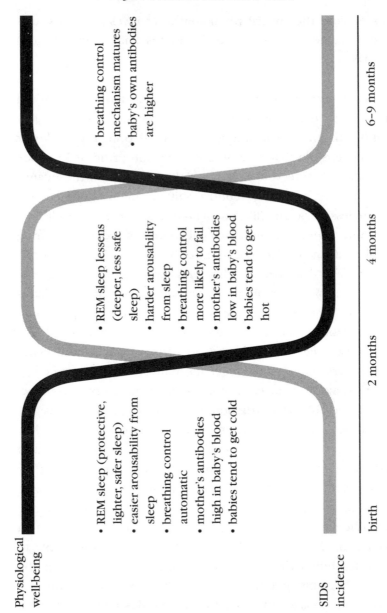

Physiological well-being

- REM sleep (protective, lighter, safer sleep)
- easier arousability from sleep
- breathing control automatic
- mother's antibodies high in baby's blood
- babies tend to get cold

- REM sleep lessens (deeper, less safe sleep)
- harder arousability from sleep
- breathing control more likely to fail
- mother's antibodies low in baby's blood
- babies tend to get hot

- breathing control mechanism matures
- baby's own antibodies are higher

SIDS incidence

birth   2 months   4 months   6–9 months

The Dip

Babies' hearts beat differently. Some infants show less stable nervous system control of their heart rates during the age they are at highest risk for SIDS.[102] In fact, new studies of infants who died of SIDS while being electronically monitored show that in some infants their heart-rate control fails before their breathing control does.[111] So, in a way, some infants enter the vulnerable period of the dip with two strikes against them, one in the heart, the other in the lungs.

Babies sleep differently. During the dip, babies shift from lighter sleep to deeper sleep. Parents may be delighted their babies are sleeping "better," yet this is actually a time when babies may not sleep safer. The very maturational process that enables babies to sleep deeper may also predispose them to SIDS. In the first two months, babies spend most of their sleeping time in a state called REM (rapid eye movement) sleep, or active sleep. During REM sleep an infant is more easily aroused, so that respiratory control systems are less likely to fail. Between two and four months, babies start to spend more time in non-REM sleep — the state of deeper sleep from which the infant is less easily awakened. This depressed arousability is found in many normal infants and to a greater extent in infants at risk for SIDS.[102] The baby is thus less capable of arousal as needed during stop-breathing or other low-oxygen episodes that may occur in deep sleep.

Some of the more convincing studies linking SIDS and lack of arousability are outlined below:

• Researchers studied nearly seven thousand normal infants during the first few months of life. Sixteen of these infants later died of SIDS. Compared to the other babies studied, the SIDS infants showed unusual sleep patterns: notably, diminished arousability during sleep.[189]

- Compared with normal infants, infants at risk of SIDS showed disturbed organization of sleep states, specifically, a diminished ability to move from sleep to waking, or a diminished arousability from sleep. And, it is noteworthy, these findings were most pronounced at age two or three months — which corresponds with the peak risk period for SIDS.[87, 169]
- Infants who experienced an ALTE (apparent life-threatening event), such as being found pale and not breathing, showed less arousability from sleep.[22]
- Siblings of SIDS babies and babies who experience ALTEs showed fewer night-waking episodes. In the first few months, infants normally have frequent periods of night waking as they ascend from quiet sleep to active sleep and back into quiet sleep. Researchers have suggested that arousal from sleep may be essential for resumption of breathing in babies who have less effective self-starting mechanisms.[87]
- When normal infants under seven months were exposed to gradually diminishing levels of oxygen during deep sleep (called the "hypoxic stimulation test"), many infants failed to arouse from sleep. This failure to arouse was most pronounced around two to three months of age — the peak age of SIDS.[234] Infants at risk of SIDS showed less response to the hypoxia stimulation test than control infants. This negative response was more pronounced in babies of drug-abusing mothers.[227]
- Experimentally produced hypoxia (low blood oxygen) in animals reduced the amount of REM or active sleep and increased the amount of deep sleep, thus making the animal even more resistant to arousal because of low oxygen levels.[11]
- Infants at high risk for SIDS showed a diminished arousal response to lowered oxygen or increased carbon dioxide during chemoreceptor challenge tests. When the carbon dioxide in the environment was increased, high-risk infants took longer to awaken and required a higher carbon dioxide level to stim-

ulate breathing. These infants were also less likely to awaken as the oxygen levels in their blood decreased. They also required a lower level of oxygen in the air to initiate awakening than did infants at low risk for SIDS. This data suggests that SIDS infants showed deficient arousal responses to sleep apnea.[152] New studies show that infants often grow out of the abnormal arousal response after the first six months of life.[72]

After six months of age, cardiorespiratory control systems are more mature and less influenced by the state of sleep, and the risk of SIDS from failure of these mechanisms is reduced.[11, 194] (For more detailed information on sleep physiology and its implications for SIDS, see Chapter 8, "Give Your Baby a Safe Sleeping Environment.")

Babies fight infection differently.   The infant's ability to fight infection is lowest during the dip months, when the incidence of SIDS is the highest. Newborns lack the ability to produce certain immunoglobulins, or infection-fighting antibodies, but are born with a rich supply of these molecular infection fighters, transferred from the mother through the placenta before birth. These antibodies get used up over the first six to nine months, during which time an infant's body learns to manufacture its own antibodies. Between two and four months antibody protection is at a low point; levels of the mother's antibodies in the baby's blood are decreasing, and the levels of antibodies made by the baby are still low. One way in which breastfeeding may help to protect against SIDS is by filling in this antibody gap. Mother's milk provides the infant with antibodies while baby's own supply is low.

Babies adjust to temperature differently.   In the first two months, infants' temperature-regulating mechanisms focus on releasing heat, so an infant of this age is more likely to be too cold than to be too warm. Around two to three months of age the body's thermostatic focus shifts to heat conservation. As a new-born was prone to get cold, a four-month-old is prone to get hot. One reason for possible overheating is that babies older than ten weeks tend to *increase* their metabolic rate in response to infec-tion, thus producing more heat; in younger babies, the metabolic rate tends to *decrease* during an infection. As I will discuss fully in Chapter 9, overheating can lead to breathing problems.

So, the first month or two of a baby's life may be considered a *grace period*, a time of relative physiological safety. The time from two to four months of age seems to be a period of *physio-logical vulnerability*, when an infant's breathing and immuno-logical systems are more likely to fail. By six months of age these systems are more mature and once again less likely to fail. The good news is that most infants pass through this developmen-tally vulnerable period without harm; the systems don't fail in 99.8 percent of infants. Even with the above-mentioned develop-mental quirks, the infant is a physiologically sturdy little person.

Additional hurdles during the dip: characteristics of in-fants at risk. Based on these physiological developments dur-ing the dip, it seems that all babies are at risk of SIDS from age two to four months, but some are at higher risk than others. Why? Do a small percentage of infants have one or more additional de-velopmental defects that place them in greater danger of dying? We know SIDS is highest in babies exposed to an unhealthy envi-ronment in the womb and in the home, for example, infants of mothers who smoke. SIDS is also higher in premature babies. It seems likely that at a crucial time in their development, high-risk infants have suffered some kind of insult, such as oxygen deprivation, to the systems controlling breathing. This can make their breathing mechanisms, which are already unstable at two to four months, even more unstable and more vulnerable. Their less effective breathing control mechanisms are more likely to fail than those in infants who do not experience these hazards.

Although we do not know the exact cause of these additional factors, new research suggests that infants at risk for SIDS may be different from those not at risk.[81, 84, 201] As previously described, physiological and postmortem studies comparing infants who have risk factors for SIDS with so-called "normal" infants show that some SIDS babies display the following characteristics:

- even less ability to arouse from sleep if their breathing is threatened
- more unstable breathing and more apnea during sleep
- less stable control of heart rates
- signs (postmortem) of low-oxygen damage to the areas of the nervous system that control breathing

However, most infants dying of SIDS do not show these findings, and most normal and at-risk infants who show these findings do not go on to die of SIDS. Nevertheless, there is enough research to conclude that some infants who go on to die of SIDS enter the world *physiologically disadvantaged* in terms of cardiorespiratory control. Thus it seems that SIDS could be considered a *developmental disability,* a deficiency of respiratory control that fails at a critical time when risky shifts are taking place in an infant's control of breathing.

But where is the "defect"? SIDS has not yet been traced to a single bunch of defective cells hidden in an obscure organ, or to an imbalance in a certain hormone, or to one single aberrant nerve pathway. If a single mechanism were at fault, the cause of SIDS would probably have already been discovered. Current knowledge suggests that SIDS is a syndrome of many causes. Yet,

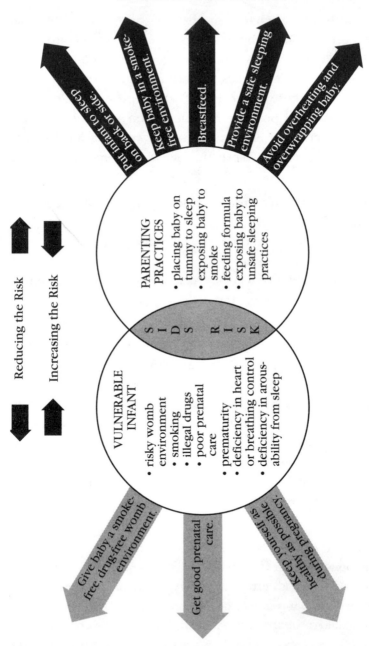

Reducing the Risk

Increasing the Risk

Put infant to sleep on back or side.

Keep baby in a smoke-free environment.

Breastfeed.

Provide a safe sleeping environment.

Avoid overheating and overwrapping baby.

PARENTING PRACTICES
- placing baby on tummy to sleep
- exposing baby to smoke
- feeding formula
- exposing baby to unsafe sleeping practices

S I D S   R I S K

VULNERABLE INFANT
- risky womb environment
- smoking
- illegal drugs
- poor prenatal care
- prematurity
- deficiency in heart or breathing control
- deficiency in arousability from sleep

Give baby a smoke-free, drug-free womb environment.

Get good prenatal care.

Keep yourself as healthy as possible during pregnancy.

The more you pull these circles apart, the lower the risk of SIDS.

the research discussed above strongly suggests that the basic defect in SIDS is a defective breathing control center, a sort of biological computer that resides at the base of the brain that automatically controls breathing and possibly heart rates.

In an infant with an unstable cardiorespiratory control center, perhaps one environmental challenge, say, overheating, wouldn't matter; perhaps not even two would cause harm, for example, a respiratory infection on top of overheating. Yet one more hazard, such as prone sleeping, may tip the scale toward failure of cardiorespiratory control. Even environmental hazards that would be considered harmless individually, for example, a stuffy nose, an overheated room, and a cold, may, all together, endanger the infant. One study in Los Angeles showed an increase in SIDS on days when the smog level (namely, carbon monoxide) was high.[100] Perhaps infants at low risk are able to withstand more challenges to their breathing than are infants at high risk who already have one or two strikes (for example, passive smoking or prematurity) against them. This is why I take the approach of offering parents many seemingly minor changes in care-giving practices, hoping they will all add up to saving little lives.

The two phases of risk. Becoming vulnerable to SIDS can be viewed as a two-phase process. The first phase occurs during *prenatal* growth, in which the infant may be exposed to an unhealthy womb environment (mother smokes or takes drugs and has no prenatal care) or be born prematurely. These prenatal factors (and/or a developmental quirk that simply occurs by chance) may determine whether or not the infant enters the world with a defective breathing control system and, thus, a higher risk of SIDS. Next is the *postnatal* phase, in which the environment the infant lives in over the next six months further influences the risk of SIDS.

Two-Phase Development of SIDS Risk

Prenatal Environment		Postnatal Environment		Risk of SIDS
Low Risk		*Low Risk*		
born at term mother doesn't smoke or use drugs	+	breastfed smoke and drug free safe sleeping proper medical care socioeconomically advantaged	=	lowest risk of SIDS
Low Risk		*High Risk*		
born at term mother doesn't smoke or use drugs	+	formula fed parents smoke and/or use drugs unsafe sleeping limited medical care socioeconomically disadvantaged	=	medium risk of SIDS
High Risk		*Low Risk*		
born preterm mother smokes or uses drugs	+	breastfed smoke and drug free safe sleeping proper medical care socioeconomically advantaged	=	medium risk of SIDS
High Risk		*High Risk*		
born preterm mother smokes or uses drugs	+	formula fed parents smoke and/or use drugs unsafe sleeping limited medical care socioeconomically disadvantaged	=	highest risk of SIDS

AN OVERVIEW OF THIS SIDS HYPOTHESIS AND MY PROPOSED RISK-REDUCTION PROGRAM

The problem. During the first six months of life, all infants are vulnerable to breathing difficulties during sleep, yet some infants are more vulnerable than others. If we assume that, besides this usual developmental vulnerability, some infants have a deficiency of cardiorespiratory control and a diminished arousability during sleep, then any parenting practice that enhances an infant's cardiorespiratory control and arousability during sleep will reduce the risk of SIDS.

SIDS seems to be an interaction of many physiological and environmental factors. The more of these factors a particular infant has, the more that infant is at risk for SIDS. The infant with many risk factors is more vulnerable than the infant with few risk factors. (See table on page 44.)

The solution. Consider the two circles shown on page 42, the one on the left showing the features of an infant vulnerable to SIDS. Some infants in this circle may have only one or two risk factors, while other infants (those at higher risk of SIDS) may have many risk factors. The second circle represents postnatal factors that can increase the risk of SIDS. The more risk factors (pre- and postnatal) the infant has, the more these circles overlap and the higher the SIDS risk. The more these circles are pulled apart by following the parenting practices suggested in this risk-reduction program, the lower the risk of SIDS becomes. Each additional risk-lowering practice pulls the circles farther apart.

The more vulnerable the infant, the more risk-reduction practices are needed. In some infants one or two of these risk-lowering factors would be powerful enough alone to prevent SIDS, but put many of these parenting practices together and you have an added effect to further reduce the SIDS risk.

Baby under construction. Think of an infant's developing cardiorespiratory control center as like an automobile engine under construction. You want to identify all the steps along the assembly line in which you can lessen the chances of the engine failing. First, you build it right. You don't use faulty materials or screws that don't fit. Similarly, a pregnant woman doesn't expose her developing infant to poisons like smoke and harmful drugs. During the assembly process, you have frequent quality-control checks. In the same way, an expectant mother seeks prenatal care. After the engine is built and running, you protect it from malfunction by using the right fuel and following the recommended maintenance schedule. Similarly, a new mother breast-feeds her infant and takes him for periodic well-baby checkups.

But despite our best efforts, mechanical engines (and biological systems) break down from time to time. A wise car owner knows his engine: a change in the way it sounds may indicate impending malfunction. He makes the adjustments he can and seeks mechanical help at the first suggestion of trouble. A wise mother knows her infant, is aware of environmental changes that may affect her baby's well-being, and fine-tunes her care-giving accordingly. She seeks medical advice when needed. With all this special attention along the way, both the engine and the baby have a better chance of achieving extended mileage.

WHAT IF YOU CAN'T DO ALL OF THE RISK-REDUCTION SUGGESTIONS?

There may be medical circumstances or lifestyle decisions that prevent you from implementing all seven steps of the risk-reduction program. For example, your baby may be born prematurely despite good prenatal care, your baby may refuse to sleep on her back or side, or, despite professional help, breastfeeding may be unsuccessful. The good news is that if some of these risk-reduction factors aren't practiced, others may compensate. For example, SIDS is rare in Asian countries, even where breastfeeding rates are low, and, at least by our standards, mothers are economically disadvantaged. Yet in these cultures, mothers seldom smoke around their babies, safe sleeping practices are observed, and infants are closely supervised and in nearly constant physical contact with an adult caregiver. Granted, ideal parenting practices may be unfeasible for all parents all the time; nevertheless, because infant lives are at stake, I present what I believe to be the ideal, supporting my beliefs with as much research as I can find and adding a touch of common sense. The rest is up to you.

By understanding the factors that make all infants vulnerable to SIDS, and some more vulnerable than others, parents can know when it is crucial to intervene in the assembly line of growth and development in order to help their infant pass through the developmental dip unharmed.

THE SEVEN-STEP SIDS PREVENTION PROGRAM

In light of new research, SIDS should no longer be considered a mysterious cloud that hangs over cribs and causes babies to take their last breath. Armed with a new understanding of SIDS, parents can at least take partial control of their parenting practices to reduce their worry and reduce the risk. You can make a difference and lower your baby's chances of dying of SIDS whether your baby is at risk or not. Here are the seven risk-lowering steps in my SIDS prevention program:

1. Give your baby a healthy womb environment.
2. Do not allow smoke around your baby — pre- or postnatally.
3. Put your baby to sleep on her back or side, not on her stomach.
4. Breastfeed your baby.
5. Give your baby a safe sleeping environment.
6. Avoid overheating your baby during sleep.
7. Practice the "high-touch" style of attachment parenting.

Now let's learn how to make the seven-step risk-reduction program work for you.

II

Preventing SIDS: A Seven-Step Program

In Part 1 you learned that SIDS seems to be caused by a combination of many factors: immature development of cardiorespiratory control mechanisms, defective arousability from sleep in response to breathing difficulties, medical conditions that compromise breathing, and unsafe sleeping practices. Therefore, this SIDS risk-reduction program is designed to meet the following goals:

- *to enhance the overall neurological development of the baby, especially the neural mechanisms that control breathing and arousability from sleep*
- *to enhance the awareness of the parents to subtle changes in their baby*
- *to improve the overall health of the baby, especially the breathing systems*
- *to create a safe sleeping environment*
- *to minimize factors that contribute to SIDS risk conditions*

4

Step One: Give Your Baby a Healthy Womb Environment

Prematurity and low birthweight constitute two of the highest risk factors for SIDS. For a three-pound baby, the risk for SIDS is ten times that of a nine-pound baby. Even babies who are delivered at term but have lower than normal birthweights (called "small-for-date infants" or "infants with intrauterine growth retardation") have an increased SIDS risk. The increased risk and the fact that premature infants show more episodes of irregular breathing and stop-breathing incidents (called apnea) are possibly because the respiratory control center in these infants is immature. So, the closer the baby gets to being mature, the lower the risk of SIDS. Although the SIDS risk in premature babies is higher, the good news is that 99 percent of premature infants don't die of SIDS and that mothers of premature babies who take good prenatal care of themselves and practice the rest of the SIDS prevention tips mentioned in this book can reduce their risk of losing their baby to SIDS. While prematurity is not always preventable, here are some practical ways you can increase your chances of giving your baby the best prenatal start.

GET GOOD PRENATAL CARE

Babies whose mothers get the least prenatal care have the highest risk of preterm birth and therefore SIDS. Just as well-baby care is important after birth, periodic checkups during pregnancy give your in-the-womb baby the best chance of a healthy start. During prenatal checkups your healthcare provider will monitor your health, counsel you on nutrition and exercise, check the growth and health of your baby, and offer you advice on creating the healthiest womb environment for your baby. Some of the conditions that cause diminished uterine blood flow, such as toxemia and high blood pressure, can occur even in expectant mothers who take good care of themselves, but these problems have not been associated with an increase in the risk of SIDS.[97]

FEED YOUR BABY RIGHT BY FEEDING YOURSELF RIGHT

Good nutrition during pregnancy lowers the risk of SIDS in two ways: it lowers the risk of prematurity, and it prevents anemia. With anemia, there are fewer red blood cells to carry oxygen to the baby. Anything that lowers oxygen to the baby increases the risk of SIDS, probably by harming the development of the baby's respiratory control system in the brain. The risk of SIDS is compounded in an anemic mother who also smokes. (For nutritional advice during pregnancy, consult *The Birth Book*.[198])

GROW YOUR BABY IN A SMOKE-FREE, DRUG-FREE WOMB

Taking illegal drugs and smoking while pregnant increase the risk of SIDS in two ways: First, these harmful habits increase the chances of your baby being born prematurely. Second, these pollutants, primarily by decreasing oxygen supply to developing tissues, can harm baby's brain, specifically the respiratory control center that regulates breathing. The harmful effects of smoking around baby, pre- and postnatally, are discussed in Chapter 5.

The risk of SIDS increases eight times in infants of substance-abusing mothers (abbreviated as ISAM) and as much as twenty times in infants of opiate-abusing mothers.[46, 108] Babies exposed to opiates or cocaine in utero are more likely to be born prematurely or to be developmentally retarded.[232] Researchers believe that drugs such as opiates and cocaine harm developing babies by constricting blood vessels in the placenta, thus reducing oxygen supply to the preborn baby — a suffocation effect similar to that caused by nicotine. As a result, the cardiorespiratory control centers may develop abnormally and are more likely to fail. How much of the increased risk of SIDS in drug-abusing mothers is due to the damage by the drug itself and how much is caused by the unhealthy socioeconomic environment is unknown, though both factors probably play a part. Substance-abusing mothers often fail to obtain adequate prenatal care. In fact, enrolling drug-abusing pregnant women in prenatal-care programs has been shown to reduce the incidence of SIDS in their babies.[14]

ISAM often show the following breathing abnormalities:

• abnormal breathing patterns, such as apnea, during sleep
• impaired breathing responses to increased carbon dioxide and decreasing oxygen
• more unstable breathing
• impaired arousal from sleep in response to a challenge, such as low oxygen
• abnormal breathing control during sleep
• abnormal nervous system control of their heart rates and more irregular heart rates

IS SIDS A SOCIAL DISEASE?

SIDS is much more likely to happen to babies born into disadvantaged homes. There is a variety of reasons for this: Disadvantaged mothers are less likely to give their babies a healthy womb environment in which to develop; their babies are less likely to be breastfed or receive adequate medical care; and their infants are more likely to be exposed to unsafe sleeping practices (the majority of infant deaths caused by unsafe sleeping environments are from homes with substandard living conditions).

So, if social conditions were improved, could SIDS incidence be lowered in economically or socially disadvantaged families? Yes. While inadequate mothering is certainly not the cause of SIDS, it may be a contributing factor in those infants already at physiological risk. SIDS is higher among infants with less skilled mothers. An interesting study in Sheffield, England, showed that improving mothering skills decreased the risk of SIDS.[35, 36] Researchers selected a group of high-risk-for-SIDS infants from a total of fifteen thousand babies. They divided these high-risk babies into two groups: One group received extra postnatal follow-up exams and biweekly home visits by a public health nurse. The mothers in the special-attention group also received education in mothering skills, nutrition, hygiene, and recognizing when their infants were sick. The second group received no special attention. The rate of SIDS was more than three times higher in the group who received no special attention — 10.6 per thousand compared to 3.2 per thousand in the special-attention group.

Better health for all babies. Some states are finally paying attention to the fact that healthy mothers are more likely to deliver healthy babies. For example, Florida's successful Improved Pregnancy Outcome and Healthy Start programs have made it possible for all pregnant women to receive adequate pre-

INFANT HOME MONITORING: WHO AND HOW LONG?

If your baby displays any symptoms associated with increased worry of SIDS (usually, an observed, prolonged apneic episode — a stop-breathing episode accompanied by a low-heart rate alarm in the newborn nursery or witnessed by parents or a caregiver while the baby is asleep, in which the infant is pale, limp, or has a color change that scares them — termed an apparent life-threatening event), your doctor may suggest, after a thorough medical evaluation, a home apnea monitor. This portable, battery-operated medical device, about the size of a lunch box, monitors the baby's heart rate and breathing during sleep. If a stop-breathing episode exceeds the setting for apnea duration or falls below a preset heart-rate level, the monitor will alarm to alert the parents to check on their baby. Newer monitors contain a computer that records heart rate and breathing continuously. These records are stored in its memory and can be later retrieved or reviewed by your doctor. This information can shed light on what happened within a few minutes prior to a stop-breathing or a low-heart rate episode.

Called "documented monitoring," this new technology is leading to a deeper understanding of the complex physiology in baby's heart and breathing control in the short period before a life-threatening event. These monitors also give us a better understanding of what is normal and what leads to breathing problems. Documented monitoring has also increased compliance, keeping parents from getting fed up with the false alarms that ruin everybody's sleep. (These monitors help identify the causes of false alarms and correct them before parents abandon their use.) In fact, documented monitoring is the new standard, because it gives doctors and parents more meaningful information and is more cost-effective.

A coming attraction in infant monitoring technology is a tiny clip that fits over baby's large toe and monitors the oxygen saturation in the blood. This physiological information is the most informative; if the oxygen saturation in baby's blood does not diminish significantly when the alarm goes off, it means that the alarm sounding is not necessarily significant. As of this writing, because of the fragility and bulkiness of the equipment, the use of oxygen measuring along with infant monitoring is not routine.

Professionals have mixed feelings about monitors. There is no statistical evidence that monitors have reduced the incidence of SIDS. Yet, statistics are little consolation to parents, who usually want monitors. What if their baby is that statistically insignificant one in a million who will be saved by a monitor? The infant home monitoring dilemma is much like the electronic fetal monitoring (EFM) controversy. Statistically, EFM during labor has not shown to yield healthier babies, yet many obstetricians attest to lives having been saved by EFM. Likewise with infant monitors, there are enough stories with happy endings to keep monitors in bedrooms for a long time.

Often the reason for monitoring an infant with a slightly higher risk of SIDS is questionable, and parents often need the monitor more than the baby does. Because infant monitoring is so entrenched in the public mind as a critical element in any risk-reduction program, it is likely to be on the scene for a long time. It would be unethical to do a controlled study, taking one group of infants and placing them on home monitors, and another group and placing them on dummy (disconnected) monitors. Parents want to know that they are doing everything possible for their baby. Who can argue with them?

Be aware that life is not always rosy with the infant attached to the monitor. False alarms occur, often due to wires falling off or being jiggled. Around 90 percent of alarms are "false." Parents' sleep is often interrupted. One reason why infant monitors may save lives is that this technology is a constant reminder to the parents of their infant's vulnerability, and therefore they are more vigilant. And life can be just a bit more complicated. Parents with a monitored baby find that maintaining the equipment is time-consuming. They also come to expect comments and questions, such as the one a six-year-old visitor asked one of my patients: "Ma'am, is your baby battery-operated?"

Currently there is a nationwide investigation called the CHIME (Collaborative Home Infant Monitoring Evaluation) study designed to assess who should use monitors. The study also hopes to assess how long monitors should be employed and what type of monitors should be used, as well as what the normal variations on infant breathing patterns are. Parents and healthcare providers hope this study will yield information that leads to improved technology and to more selective use of infant home monitors.

As of now, home monitoring is recommended for newborns who have shown stop-breathing/low-heart rate episodes in the hospital, and infants at any age who have experienced an ALTE (apparent life-threatening event). Whether to monitor subsequent siblings of SIDS babies is controversial; the National Institute of Health committee of experts has recommended *against* routine monitoring of SIDS siblings. But this is an individual judgment call, usually based upon the parents' wishes. As part of the home monitoring program, parents are instructed in CPR and simple methods to restart normal breathing, which usually requires only gently jostling or awakening the baby.

When to wean a baby off an infant monitor is a combined medical and parental decision, based upon a few weeks of no real alarm events while baby is asleep. Home monitoring is typically discontinued around seven months of age or once the parents are comfortable with the idea of their baby sleeping without a monitor. As a reminder, electronic home monitoring is no substitute for parental vigilance and the other risk-lowering factors mentioned in this book.

natal care. As a result, Florida's infant mortality rate from *all* causes has fallen 30 percent over the past ten years.

Healthy Start programs, such as the one in Florida, are proving successful at lowering the SIDS rate, even for babies born with risk factors. These programs involve more than doling out formula and food stamps. They provide *education* and *support,* specifically, encouraging families to quit smoking and stop taking drugs; encouraging and educating mothers in the art and importance of breastfeeding; offering classes that teach parents the art of attachment parenting (see Chapter 10 for how attachment parenting lowers the risk of SIDS); teaching parents how to recognize when their babies are sick; making sure families have access to medical care; and, finally, teaching parenting skills, such as babywearing (see page 159), that increase parents' overall knowledge and awareness of their babies.

5

Step Two: Thank You for Not Smoking

One of the most significant risk factors for SIDS — and one that mothers can do something about — is smoking when their babies are in the womb or in the same room. Studies show that exposure to cigarette smoking at least doubles the risk of SIDS.[85, 192] In the collaborative study of eight hundred SIDS infants, 70 percent of the mothers of these infants smoked during pregnancy; and investigators concluded that maternal smoking during pregnancy more than tripled the SIDS risk.[95, 119] The risk of SIDS increases proportionally to the number of cigarettes mother smokes.[147] Heavy maternal smoking (more than twenty cigarettes a day) increases the SIDS risk fivefold. If mother and father smoke, the risk of baby dying of SIDS *doubles,* compared with maternal smoking alone.[182f] Anything that retards infant development, interferes with infant breathing, or lessens maternal sensitivity increases the risk of SIDS. Smoking around babies does all three.

HOW SMOKING HARMS BABIES IN THE WOMB

How much of the increased SIDS risk from cigarette smoking is due to the smoke itself and how much is due to the smoker is difficult to tell. It's probably a combination of both. The mother who smokes during pregnancy and/or around her baby after birth

LONG-TERM EFFECTS OF MATERNAL SMOKING AND CHILDREN'S BRAIN DEVELOPMENT

Studies have shown the following correlations between mothers who smoke during pregnancy, especially heavy smoking (more than one pack a day), and the growth and brain development of their children.* Children of mothers who smoke during pregnancy are more likely to show the following:[119, 166, 182]

- decreased newborn Apgar scores (if smoking more than one pack a day)
- decreased mental performance scoring at age one year
- decreased academic performance scores in the school-age child
- reduced IQ
- shorter stature (by one to two centimeters)
- smaller head circumference as infants
- increased learning difficulties (children were 25 percent more likely to have learning disabilities if their mother smoked more than twenty cigarettes a day)
- increased hyperactivity
- increased behavioral problems

---

*Studies on the long-term effects of smoking during pregnancy on children's mental and physical development did not all agree. Some showed slight or no adverse effects. The above conclusions represent the general consensus of outcome studies.

is less likely to take good care of herself prenatally, less likely to breastfeed, and less likely to practice the overall style of attachment parenting that I believe lowers the risk of SIDS. Consider the physiological effects of smoking on you and your baby.

It retards growth. Smoking stunts the growth of the developing fetus. Nicotine narrows the uterine blood vessels, thus reducing blood flow to the baby. Also, smoking puts the oxygen blocker carbon monoxide into the blood that nourishes baby.[233] Carbon monoxide robs oxygen from the baby. Levels of carbon monoxide have been measured at six to seven times higher in the blood of pregnant women who smoke. Carbon monoxide levels in cigarette smoke resemble that of automobile exhaust.[182j] Smoking thus reduces the oxygen supply to the infant in the womb, in effect, slightly smothering the defenseless baby.

It retards brain development. Nicotine has been shown experimentally to retard fetal brain growth in animals.[157] The developing brain is particularly vulnerable to low levels of oxygen, and immaturity of the brain center that regulates breathing could contribute to SIDS (see page 33). Recent studies of smoking mothers' infants who died in the womb provide insight into how exposure to smoking may injure developing brains. Besides causing neurological damage by lessening oxygen supply to the developing brain, nicotine may be directly poisonous to areas of the brain involved with heart and breathing functions and arousal from sleep.[119] Also, infants whose mothers smoked during pregnancy are more likely to have diminished arousal from sleep in response to a low-oxygen challenge.[133]

It impairs breathing after birth. Mothers who smoke at least half a pack of cigarettes a day during pregnancy are nearly three times more likely to have babies with mucus-blocked airways or episodes of apnea.

It increases the likelihood of prematurity. The risk of SIDS goes up as baby's birthweight and gestational age go down. Babies of smoking mothers end up being smaller (due to intrauterine growth retardation), and smoking increases the risk of complications of pregnancy that lead to prematurity: premature rupture of fetal membranes, placenta previa, and premature detachment of the placenta.

Passive smoking also harms the baby. When expectant mothers are exposed to smoke from other people's cigarettes, their babies are also exposed. One study showed that a pregnant woman's exposure to smoke for at least two hours a day doubles her risk of delivering a low-birthweight baby. While older studies claimed no increased SIDS risk if the father smoked, newer stud-

When mother smokes, baby smokes.

ies report a higher risk of SIDS if the father smokes.[85, 121] Demand that your husband and coworkers respect the life inside your womb. If your job requires working in a smoke-contaminated environment while pregnant, know that this is a proven health hazard to your baby and is grounds for reassignment to a baby-healthy environment. As a testimony to the wisdom of the body, many mothers find they have an aversion to being around cigarette and cigar smoke (and to drinking alcohol) while pregnant. Listen to the warnings of your body and hundreds of medical studies:

HARMFUL EFFECTS OF SMOKING ON MOTHERS AND BABIES

Smoking has the following effects on mothers and babies:

- Increased infertility (smoking could account for 10 percent of infertility problems in mothers)[182]
- Increased risk of ectopic pregnancy[182b]
- Increased risk of placenta previa[182d]
- Increased risk of premature separation of the placenta[182d]
- Increased risk of placental abnormalities (known as "smoker's placenta")[130, 178, 182d]
- Increased risk of problem pregnancies (e.g., pre-eclampsia)[182d]
- Increased risk of prematurity and intrauterine growth retardation[182d]
- *20 percent* increased risk of the newborn dying at birth;[31, 150] *35 percent* increase if mother smokes more than thirty-five cigarettes a day[154]
- Increased risk of respiratory infections in infant[182c]
- Increased risk of SIDS by two to five times[95, 182f]

Don't expose yourself and your baby to smoke while pregnant. Legally, you have a right to work in a smoke-free environment.

HOW POSTNATAL SMOKING INCREASES THE RISK OF SIDS

Suppose you were about to take your baby into a room when you noticed a sign that read: WARNING, THIS ROOM CONTAINS POISONOUS GASES OF AROUND FOUR THOUSAND CHEMICALS, SOME OF WHICH HAVE BEEN LINKED

TO CANCER AND LUNG DAMAGE AND ARE ESPECIALLY HARMFUL TO THE BREATH-ING PASSAGES OF YOUNG INFANTS. "I certainly wouldn't take my baby in there," you would conclude. Yet that's exactly what happens when you take your baby into a room frequented by smokers. "But we always sit in the no-smoking area of public places," you add. This is helpful, but not enough. Having a no-smoking area is like trying to chlorinate half a swimming pool. Pollutants travel through the air. "But I only smoke outside," you rationalize. Also helpful, but not enough. Smoke sticks to clothing and hair. When your baby nestles on your shoulder with his nose on your smoke-contaminated clothing and near your hair, your baby inhales pollutants.

Parents have a right to fume over the poisonous gases that come from a cigarette or cigar burning in their baby's presence. Among the many toxic ingredients in cigarette smoke are the oxygen blocker carbon monoxide;[234] benzene, a potential carcinogen; ammonia; hydrogen cyanide, which is used in making rat poison; formaldehyde; and of course, nicotine. Here are some of the effects.

It bothers little breathers. Any poison that deprives the infant of oxygen increases the risk of SIDS. Cigarette and cigar smoke deprive the infant of oxygen, which could interfere with development of the brain center that controls breathing. When the body is chronically deprived of oxygen it tries to compensate by increasing the production of a chemical that facilitates oxygen transport, called 2,3 DPG. Levels of this substance have been found to be higher in children exposed to smoke, indicating they are trying to compensate for chronic oxygen deprivation.[163] Cotinine, the main chemical produced when the body breaks down nicotine, has been found in the blood of babies exposed to passive smoke, proof that harmful chemicals enter babies' bodies from cigarette or cigar smoke in the environment. Nicotine, cotinine, and another nicotine byproduct, thiocyanate, have also

DOES SMOKING *CAUSE* SIDS?

Critics of the smoking and SIDS studies argue that the research shows a correlation, but that that does not prove causation. I take issue with this defense, as do others.[182] This argument has kept possibly life-saving labels off cigarette advertising. While policymakers haggle, babies are dying. Consider this evidence that smoking causes SIDS. Short of absolute experimental proof, researchers have come up with the following criteria for upgrading a "correlation" to a "cause":

The strength of the studies.   Critics argue that statistical studies are flawed. True, but statistical studies are seldom perfect. And, critics claim, mothers who smoke also tend to have other SIDS risk factors.

The consistency of the studies.   Ten out of eleven studies show a correlation between maternal smoking and SIDS. All show a correlation between smoking and damage to the fetus or infant. All five studies that looked at this relationship found that the SIDS risk increases with the number of cigarettes smoked daily.

The biologic plausibility of the claim; in other words, does it agree with common sense?   Certainly exposing the developing infant's brain, heart, and lungs to chemicals that rob oxygen from the fetus and damage the placenta can't be good for baby.

Read the studies mentioned throughout this chapter, add a bit of common sense, and you will come to the conclusion that smoking can kill babies.

If both parents smoke, baby's SIDS risk is 3½ times greater than if neither parent smokes.

If mother smokes, but father doesn't, baby's risk is 2 times greater.

If father smokes, but mother doesn't, baby's risk is 1½ times greater.[85, 121, 182]

been found in the blood of breastfed infants whose mothers smoke.[182] (Whether these poisons enter the baby via mothers' milk or secondhand smoke is uncertain.[121]) The blood levels of the nicotine byproducts were proportional to the number of cigarettes smoked by the mother.

It hurts little hearts. Besides being harmful to growing lungs, smoking may harm growing hearts. Levels of HDL, best known as the "good cholesterol" that may protect from heart disease, were lower in children of smoking parents. In addition, researchers have found high levels of cotinine in the fluid around the hearts of some infants who died of SIDS.[156] Smoke toxins have also been implicated in depressing the automatic regulation of heart rates.[60]

It injures little brains.   Previously I mentioned how smoking prenatally may retard the growth of baby's brain. It appears that the brain of a baby of a smoker doesn't fare much better outside the womb. In experiments, nicotine acts as a breathing stimulant to animals who are breathing normally. But as soon as their breathing is compromised, nicotine seems to depress the compensatory breathing control mechanisms in the brain that should return the animal's breathing to normal.[157] It is possible that a smoking mother's infant whose breathing is already compromised, say, from a cold, could fail to restart breathing because of the effects of nicotine.

Smoking shortens lives — young and old.

SHOULD CIGARETTES BE LABELED "HAZARDOUS TO INFANT HEALTH?"

Why isn't there such a warning on cigarette packages like there is against drinking alcohol while pregnant? Health authorities refuse to do this because, they claim, there is no proven cause-and-effect relationship between smoking and infant damage and death — only a statistical one. Sounds like the same feeble excuse that delayed the "smoking causes cancer" labeling.

I would like to see warnings such as SMOKING KILLS BABIES or SMOKING RETARDS INFANTS on every cigarette pack. As a case in point, Dr. Peter Fleming, a prominent SIDS researcher, told me that he tried to get such blunt labels put on cigarette packs in the United Kingdom; yet because of political pressure, the government would allow only a misleading, cigarette industry–backed warning like SMOKING MAY CAUSE BABIES TO BE BORN SMALLER. Tobacco companies spend millions to research the potential impact of warnings. They concluded that mothers who smoke might be delighted with such a warning because they would think (erroneously) it was easier to birth smaller babies.[60] There are warnings on alcohol bottles that drinking during pregnancy could cause birth defects, yet the risk of SIDS is 3.4 times greater from smoking than from consuming alcohol while pregnant.[95] I propose that enough evidence exists today to merit putting on each pack of cigarettes and on all tobacco ads a warning label like RESEARCH HAS DETERMINED THAT SMOKING WHILE PREGNANT OR AROUND INFANTS INCREASES THE RISK OF SIDS.

RESEARCH HAS DETERMINED THAT SMOKING WHILE PREGNANT OR AROUND INFANTS INCREASES THE RISK OF SIDS.

It blocks little noses. The nasal passages of babies are particularly sensitive to smoke and other irritants and allergens. Also, some babies are obligate nose breathers, meaning they insist on breathing through their nose and, unlike adults, do not switch to mouth breathing if their noses are blocked. Nasal passages that are stuffy and blocked because of smoke could compromise baby's breathing.

The lower respiratory tract is lined with tiny filaments, called "cilia," which wave back and forth to clear mucus from the airway passages and help keep them open. Smoke paralyzes these cilia, leaving the increased mucus that is secreted during colds and allergies to clog the air passages. Children of smoking parents have two to three times more doctor visits because of respiratory infections. Respiratory viruses are frequently found at postmortem examinations of SIDS infants.[240] Respiratory infections within two weeks of death have been implicated in setting up a baby for SIDS.

HOW SMOKING HAMPERS MOTHERING

If the above findings aren't enough to convince you to puff no more, consider this research.

It interferes with natural mothering. Lack of breastfeeding is a risk factor for SIDS. Mothers who smoke tend either not to breastfeed or to wean earlier, and to have more breastfeeding problems, perhaps because smoking suppresses lactation by interfering with the milk-producing hormones.[143, 182g] Studies of breastfeeding mothers who smoked showed that the nicotine concentration in their breast milk was three times higher than in their blood, suggesting that not only can babies inhale tobacco poisons, they can drink them as well.[129] Also alarming is a finding that mothers who smoke have lower levels of prolactin, the hormone that regulates milk production and

IF YOUR PREGNANT FRIEND SMOKES — WHAT YOU CAN DO

When you care enough to give healthcare advice, here is my advice: You *can* help pregnant mothers quit smoking, as the following studies show.

In one study, first-time pregnant mothers who smoked were divided into two groups on their prenatal visit to their healthcare provider, either an obstetrician or midwife. One group received personal compelling advice on the harmful effects of smoking on their developing infant. Fifty-eight percent of these mothers either quit or reduced smoking while pregnant. The other group of smokers received no quit-smoking advice. Only 31 percent of mothers in this group quit or reduced smoking during their pregnancy. Personal advice was the most effective; leaflet-only advice had only slight benefits. Researchers then compared the babies of mothers who quit or reduced smoking with those who didn't. The babies of the no- or reduced-smoking mothers were heavier and longer than the babies born to mothers who didn't change their smoking habits during pregnancy. The earlier mothers quit smoking during their pregnancy, the better the outcome of their infants.[182] Even though mothers who quit after four months of their pregnancy had smaller infants than early stoppers, their infants were still heavier than those who persisted to smoke throughout their pregnancy.

In another study, 27 percent of the mothers who received proper intervention counseling quit smoking during their pregnancy, compared with 3 percent who received no counseling; and the infants of mothers who quit smoking were heavier and larger.[200]

> When you offer quit-smoking advice, make it caring, yet compelling. Wimpy advice — which the mother could interpret as condoning smoking — may harm more than help.[142] The advice needs to be convincing enough to override the addiction. Try, "Mary, I am saying this to you because I care about the health of you and your baby. Smoking could retard or kill your baby. Please quit."

affects mothering behavior.[172] Diminished maternal awareness of an infant's needs has been implicated as a risk factor of SIDS, and a mother with less prolactin going through her may have less awareness of her infant, an especially worrisome situation when one considers that these infants are already compromised due to their exposure to smoke and nicotine.

At this writing at least five reputable scientific studies conclude that smoking around babies increases the risk of SIDS, and the more cigarettes the parents smoke, the higher the risk.

Normally, mothers would never do anything to deliberately harm their babies, except when addiction overrules. Your infant needs healthy lungs and healthy parents. You owe it to yourself and to your baby to stop smoking. Smoking and parenting don't mix — without a risk.

RESOURCES TO HELP STOP SMOKING

Despite the warning in the "Back to Sleep" campaign (see explanation, page 27) that smoking may increase the risk of SIDS, researchers in England found that the anti-smoking warning campaign had no impact on mothers who already smoked (though it did seem to deter some mothers from starting). Smokers followed the other SIDS risk-reduction suggestions, such as switching their baby's sleeping position from front to back, but continued to smoke. I'm surprised at these results, since normally mothers would never do anything to deliberately harm their infant. I conclude, therefore, that concerning smoking, a mother's addiction can override her intuition. When it comes to smoking, too many people still feel they'll beat the odds: "It just can't happen to me." "It just can't happen to my baby."

From this mind-set we can learn the following things: First, there must be laws to protect infants who can't help themselves and parents who can't, or won't, protect them. Also, there need to be support resources to help parents, especially mothers, quit smoking. Finally, the information on how smoking hurts babies needs to reach pre-smokers, namely teens (infants of teen mothers are at higher risk of SIDS). This tactic is being tried in New Zealand with the Kids Against SIDS campaign, in which teens are taught the hazards of smoking *before* they get pregnant or start smoking. The surgeon general's 1994 report "Preventing Tobacco Use Among Young People" concludes that if people don't start smoking as adolescents, most will never become smokers.[68]

If SIDS parents, healthcare professionals, and other concerned citizens start to scream louder than the tobacco executives, we may soon see effective warning labels, public health campaigns, and a decrease in parental smoking. Researchers estimate that if maternal smoking could be eliminated altogether, the overall infant death rate could be reduced by 10 percent and the SIDS rate by 27 percent.[86, 146, 182]

Pamphlets and information on how to quit smoking can be obtained from these resources:

American Cancer Society
1-800-227-2345

American Lung Association
1-212-315-8700

A Pregnant Woman's Guide to Quit Smoking
By Richard A. Windsor and Dianne Smith
Available at your library or from bookstores, this book contains a ten-day, twenty-step workbook on practical ways to quit smoking.

6

Step Three: Put Your Baby to Sleep on Her Back or Side

Whether to place babies to sleep on their bellies or backs has been one of the most controversial of parenting practices. Traditionally, mothers in Western cultures favored putting their babies to sleep on their stomachs (prone) for fear their babies would choke if they spit up while lying on their backs. Eastern-culture mothers, on the other hand, have traditionally placed their infants to sleep on their backs (supine) for fear they would suffocate if sleeping on their stomachs. It turns out that cultures where babies traditionally sleep on their backs have lower SIDS rates than cultures where babies sleep on their tummies.[47] New research further supports the theory that back-sleeping is safer. As discussed in Chapter 2, this important finding has led to "Back to Sleep" campaigns throughout the world. The result is that SIDS rates have fallen 40–70 percent in eight countries that instituted a national SIDS risk-reduction campaign advising parents to avoid putting their infants to sleep on their stomachs. SIDS rates have also been falling slightly in the United States following media publicity advising parents not to put their babies to sleep on their tummies.

Even though the SIDS prevention campaigns were dubbed "Back to Sleep," the campaign brochures also advised mothers to breastfeed their babies; not smoke during pregnancy or around their babies; avoid overwrapping their babies; and not overheat their babies' bedrooms. How much these other factors, in addition to back-sleeping, contributed to the dramatic decrease in SIDS rates was the next question to tackle. The Avon Project researchers found that of these four guidelines in infant-care practices, the baby's sleeping position was changed by more parents than any other factor. As noted in Chapter 5, mothers who smoked were particularly resistant to stopping. The Avon researchers did notice that fewer SIDS infants were breastfed than were bottle-fed, but they attributed this to the observation that breastfeeding mothers, because of their greater education and access to medical care, were more likely to follow the advice of healthcare professionals and put their babies to sleep on their backs. Other studies showed that while the majority of mothers interviewed said they now put their babies to sleep on their backs, the incidence of breastfeeding and maternal smoking didn't change.[216] Thus researchers concluded that the drastic decline in SIDS rates must be due primarily to putting babies to sleep on their sides or backs instead of on their stomachs.

SIDS researchers caution that back-sleeping is not a SIDS-free guarantee. In this way, the "Back to Sleep" campaign is similar to the infant carseat campaign. Both reduce the risk but, because of other factors, do not prevent all deaths. Many unanswered questions remain about the correlation between tummy-sleeping and SIDS, and changing the sleeping position from front to back may prevent, at most, only 50 percent of SIDS cases. The other half of SIDS cases require other explanations. For the time being it seems prudent to recommend that infants up to six months of age be put to sleep on their backs or sides.

BABIES WHO SHOULD SLEEP TUMMY DOWN

Be sure to check with your doctor to see if your baby has any medical conditions that necessitate front-sleeping. Babies who *should* sleep prone are the following:

- premature babies still in the hospital with respiratory problems; sleeping on the tummy increases breathing efficiency in prematures with compromised breathing, but not necessarily when their lungs are normal
- babies with small jawbones or other oral structural abnormalities that may compromise the airways when sleeping on their backs
- babies who have mucus-producing respiratory infections or profuse drooling associated with teething — *if so advised by your doctor*
- babies who are extremely restless and settle poorly unless sleeping prone
- babies who suffer from gastroesophageal reflux (GER).[174, 175] (See page 82 for proper positioning of these babies.)

QUESTIONS YOU MAY HAVE

Here are some of the most frequently asked questions about sleep positions for babies.

My mother and mother-in-law think I'm crazy to put my son to sleep on his back. They're sure he'll choke. Could he? Until recent "Back to Sleep" campaigns, conventional Western wisdom taught that babies should sleep on their stomach for fear of choking. I dutifully recorded it as my own advice to parents in my book *Nighttime Parenting,* published in 1985. But it turns out that not only is aspiration (inhaling of milk, food, or spit-up into the lungs) or choking rare, but SIDS experts no longer even consider it a possible cause of SIDS. In fact, studies show that after a change from front- to back-sleeping, there was no increase in aspiration; in fact, the problem may have even decreased.[83]

Another reason for the front-sleeping preference was the observation of mothers, confirmed by researchers, that many babies settled better, slept better, and cried less when placed to sleep on their tummies.[29, 110] It seems newborns settle better on their stomachs or sides because they feel more contained, less vulnerable to startle. And because we are a culture whose parenting practices have traditionally fostered an uninterrupted night's sleep, it seems odd to put our babies to sleep in a position that might encourage them to wake up more easily. In a 1992 survey of two thousand U.S. households 74 percent of infants usually slept prone, 14 percent slept on their sides, and 12 percent on their backs. Conventional parenting wisdom says, "Why change what works? Let sleeping babies lie." For a culture that treasures its sleep, this change will require some savvy public relations.

Some babies sleeping on their tummies also seemed to settle better and spit up less after feeding.[26, 155, 175, 226] If an infant has gastroesophageal reflux (an infant malady similar to heartburn; see page 81), it is still recommended that he sleep tummy down, at least for two hours after a feeding.[67]

Martha, my wife, believes there is another reason why babies are put to sleep on their tummies. If a mother is *putting* her baby to sleep, rather than *parenting* her to sleep (see page 104 for an explanation of the difference), the front position works better. Many babies do not like being flat on their backs when they are tired, and most babies will resist by crying when they are plunked down this way awake. When put tummy down, a baby would be more able to comfort herself off to sleep by assuming the fetal position and sucking on her fingers. A front position would also encourage a baby who does awaken to return to sleep on her own for these reasons.

A final reason for the traditional front-sleeping position is that new mothers see nurses put babies down this way in the hospital, and mothers often do what they've seen nurses do. (Also, young doctors in training see nurses place newborns to sleep on their stomachs, so they pass on this habit to the mothers in their practice, and the cycle continues.) Nurses are accustomed to putting babies to sleep on their tummies because that's what they have learned is best for premature babies or babies with breathing difficulties; the still partially collapsed lungs of some prematures tend to expand better when front-sleeping. Yet this benefit is *only* for preterm babies and others with breathing difficulties. Once babies are well and at home, the front-sleeping position is unlikely to benefit their breathing.[149, 208, 229]

How does back-sleeping decrease the risk of SIDS?

The reason for the relationship between back-sleeping and lower SIDS risk is currently unknown; and, remember, the research shows only a *correlation, not a causation.* Yet, there are several possible explanations for why back-sleeping is safer than front.

Babies awaken easier. Arousability from sleep in response to a life-threatening event is a healthy, protective mechanism and one that is thought to be diminished in infants at risk of SIDS. Back-sleepers arouse from sleep more easily and sleep less deeply than tummy-sleepers.[29, 66, 107] Mothers have observed, and research has confirmed, that infants sleep more deeply on their tummies. Yet, as we will see in Chapter 8, sleeping more deeply does not mean sleeping more safely.

Babies have less chance of getting overheated. Another reason why back-sleeping is safer is that babies lying on their

GER AND SIDS

Gastroesophageal reflux (GER), the regurgitation of stomach acids into the esophagus, has recently been implicated as a cause of SIDS and ALTEs.[144] The reflux of these irritating acids into the esophagus and/or areas near the larynx may trigger airway blockage from a laryngeal spasm or trigger reflexes that produce asthma, apnea, and/or slow heart rates.

GER may be a greater problem during slow-wave sleep, the deepest of the sleep states, which begins to appear between two and three months of age. During the slow-wave sleep, swallowing is depressed and refluxed gastric contents may stay in the esophagus for longer periods, where they can both act as an irritant and interfere with breathing.

Some degree of GER may be found in as many as 40 percent of newborns. After the age of four months, as intestinal function matures, GER occurs much less often and usually subsides by the first birthday, although some people experience varying degrees of GER all their lives. Whether SIDS and GER occur together as a coincidence or whether GER is a cause of SIDS is still debatable, and the research is conflicting. Nevertheless, many cases of ALTE have been traced to GER, so that any baby presenting with an ALTE should be evaluated for GER. (See the related SIDS story on page 177.) During my years in pediatric practice, I have been impressed with the association between GER and breathing difficulties in infants and children. I believe that minimizing GER belongs in the overall SIDS prevention package. Here's what parents can do:

1. Breastfeed your baby. GER occurs less often and is less severe in the breastfed baby (see page 97).
2. Wear your baby as often as possible in a vertical position in a baby sling. Reflux decreases when baby is upright. Gravity helps to keep the food down because the outlet from the stomach is lower than the inlet. (See "Baby-wearing and SIDS Risk Reduction," page159.)
3. Offer smaller, more frequent feedings rather than large feedings. A smaller amount of milk is less likely to be regurgitated. Also, milk acts as an antacid, which may explain why infants with GER enjoy nursing frequently.
4. Attend to crying promptly. Babies reflux more while crying.
5. Avoid sitting a sleeping baby with proven GER in an infant seat. The semireclined position can increase reflux if the stomach outlet is higher than the inlet.
6. Parents are usually advised to place babies with proven GER to sleep on their bellies,[67] with the head of the bed elevated thirty degrees. Reflux wedges and slings are available to decrease the risk of the elevated baby's slipping under the covers and becoming too hot. Some studies show this position facilitates gastric emptying.[174]
7. Don't jostle baby during and for at least thirty minutes after feeding.
8. Don't smoke around your baby. Exposure to secondhand smoke may increase GER.
9. Placing GER babies to sleep on their *right* side ensures the gastric inlet is higher than the outlet, and so gravity helps to keep the milk down.
10. Don't prop up a bottle and leave baby unsupervised during a feeding. Reflex apnea can occur during a feeding.

tummies are more likely to become overheated, and, as we shall see in Chapter 9, overheating increases the risk of SIDS. The back-lying position seems to be the preferred position if a person gets hot during sleep. Notice what you do. When you are hot, you probably turn over onto your back and spread out. Lying on your side or back leaves your face and internal organs exposed so they can radiate heat more readily than when you're on your tummy. When cold, you probably curl up on your front or side to conserve heat. Also, front-sleeping babies are more likely to slip down under their covers than those sleeping on their backs, another factor that may contribute to overheating, since a baby's prime avenue for heat loss is through the head and face. And don't forget that the head contains the respiratory control center. In the back or side position, even a baby who slipped down underneath the covers would be more likely to throw them off.[62] The contact of the cover with the face is more likely to be noticed and protested by a back-sleeping baby than the contact of the cover with the back of the head would be in a front-sleeping baby.

Babies are less likely to suffocate. Conventional thinking has always taught that suffocation is a rare cause of SIDS. Yes, babies are sturdy little persons who, even as newborns, are able to lift their heads and keep their noses clear to breathe. The often quoted "study" that even tiny infants have the ability to lift their heads and wiggle their noses clear of obstruction was not really a scientific study; it was more of an observation.[246] Yet, new insights cast doubt on the rareness of suffocation. A growing belief among SIDS researchers is that many babies presumably diagnosed as SIDS babies may in reality have died from suffocation on soft surfaces.

When sleeping facedown, a baby may press her head into the mattress or wiggle her face against a soft object. This can form a pocket of air around her face, leaving her to rebreathe her own exhaled air, which has diminished oxygen.[27, 39, 56, 113]

Babies' airways are open wider. When a baby sleeps prone, his tongue and jawbones can be pressed backward, and the soft tissues of the nose can be compressed by the weight of his face on the mattress, thereby narrowing the air passages in his throat.[208, 221, 243] Add this airway compromise to the fact that the airway is already more narrow during sleep (due to relaxation of the muscles that keep the airway open) and you have the setup for more compromise to airflow when sleeping prone.

Babies breathe more easily. If I could cast another theory into the front-sleeping arena, I would suggest that it is harder for baby to breathe with the abdomen and chest pressed against a mattress. When taking a deep breath, the front-sleeper has to lift the weight of much of his body. Back-sleeping allows the chest and the abdomen to expand freely. Studies have shown that infants have improved oxygenation and pulmonary function in the prone position if a depression has been cut in the mattress to facilitate abdominal excursions.[2, 229]

Babies are more accessible. In watching our babies sleep, I have been impressed by how much more access the baby has to the mother and the mother to the baby when baby is sleeping on her side or back rather than prone. This could be an important consideration if baby needs help.

Another theory is that the front-sleeping position may hyperextend the neck and compromise blood flow to the areas of the brain that control breathing.[48, 57, 71] This theory has received mixed reviews and is not widely accepted. A final theory is that if the infant experiences a stop-breathing episode, the infant's ability to restart breathing may be less when sleeping tummy down.

While no one knows exactly why the front-sleeping position is linked to SIDS, the overwhelming number of studies that all come to the same conclusion — front-sleeping increases the risk of SIDS — make it clear that for healthy infants supine sleep is safer.

Could sleeping on the back be dangerous?

There are certain medical conditions in which babies breathe better tummy down (see "Babies Who Should Sleep Tummy Down," page 78). If your baby has any of these conditions, be sure to consult your doctor for advice on the safest sleeping position for your baby. This position may also vary with the age and health of your baby.

What if my baby prefers sleeping on her tummy?

If baby doesn't settle well or stay on her back or side, front-sleeping is all right. Unless advised to the contrary by your doctor, it is best to let your baby sleep in a position she prefers. Also, you may find that your baby has different sleep-position preferences at different ages. After all, there is a meaningful wisdom of the body, even in a baby; if a baby repeatedly doesn't settle in a certain sleeping position, this may be a clue that this position may not be the safest for this individual baby. This is just one example of how babies often try to tell us what is in their best interest. Parents should not be afraid to listen.

Still, because of the new research, it is best to try to get baby accustomed to sleeping on her back or side. Newborn babies get in the habit of sleeping the way they are first put down. The older babies get, the more resistant they seem to be to changes in sleeping position. Newly born babies do well sleeping on their tummies, but they also do well on their sides, since both placements allow babies to assume the fetal position, which is more soothing than back-lying. Thus, if you have been putting your baby down on her stomach and now you wish to get her used to sleeping on her back or side, it may take some patient conditioning. If you've made a diligent effort to encourage back-sleeping and your baby

BACK-TO-SLEEP TRAINING

What if your baby protests any position except tummy-sleeping? Try these tips to encourage back- or side-sleeping:

1. Let the tummy-sleeper first fall asleep on her tummy; then, after she is soundly asleep, gently turn her over onto her back.
2. Rock or nurse baby to sleep in your arms or while wearing baby in a baby sling. Once baby is asleep, place her down on her back.
3. Promote the crib-sleeper to your bed (see suggested sleeping arrangement, page 110). Following this night-time upgrade, most solo-sleepers will prefer to sleep on their sides or backs for easier access to parents.
4. Don't worry if the back-sleeper persistently turns over onto her side or front to sleep. By the time babies are developmentally able to perform this flip, they are usually past the age of high risk for SIDS.
5. If, after trying all the above, your tummy-sleeper still would rather fuss than switch, consider that the sleeping disturbance for baby and family caused by persisting with an unworking sleep-position change may be a greater SIDS risk than the tummy-sleeping itself. In this case, the best you can do is provide a safe sleeping environment for your front-sleeper. Use a firm sleeping surface and survey baby's sleeping environment for potential nose-blockers. Use fitted crib sheets. Remove soft crib toys and pillows. Be sure crib bumpers, if used, are secured tightly and there are no large crevices between the mattress and crib sides or bumpers. (See related section on crib safety, page 139.)

still sleeps best on her stomach, let her, and don't fear that she is going to die of SIDS, especially if the other risk factors are not present. Studies on large numbers of babies show a *statistical* increase in SIDS if baby sleeps tummy down, but your baby is an individual. The front-sleeping risk factor for SIDS doesn't mean that you should worry every time you place your baby down to sleep. Just be sure to place her down on a safe bedding surface. (See safe bedding tips on page 140.) After all, 999 out of 1,000 tummy-sleeping infants don't die of SIDS.

Is it safer for baby to sleep on his back or side?
New Zealand studies show that SIDS is least likely to occur when babies sleep on their backs, and most likely when sleeping on their tummies.[158] Sleeping on the side falls somewhere in be-

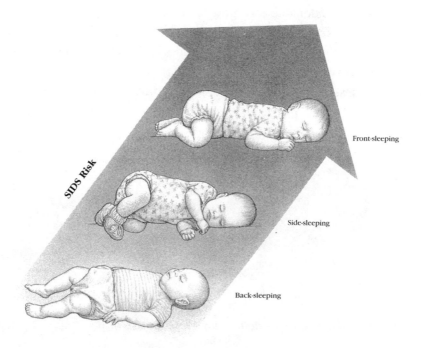

Front-sleeping

Side-sleeping

Back-sleeping

SIDS Risk

tween. This statistical difference is not enough that parents should avoid putting babies to sleep on their sides.

Sleeping on the back, however, is a more stable position than on the side. Many infants do not develop the desire or the motor capability to roll from back to tummy until around five or six months, when the risk of SIDS begins to diminish. Yet even newborns have the capability of rolling from side to back or side to tummy. While most babies under six months who are put to sleep on their tummies or backs tend to stay there, many infants who are put down to sleep on their sides will change position, most of the time rolling onto their backs rather than onto their tummies.[63] Yet the number of SIDS infants who rolled from their sides to the front position in the Avon study led experts in England[60] and New Zealand[158] to suggest that the risk of SIDS for side-sleeping may be two times that of back-sleeping. (Once again, parents should be aware that these are purely statistical findings and of questionable meaning for individuals.) At present, most authorities agree that the research only supports discouraging the front position, and that both side- and back-sleeping are safe alternatives.

To lessen the chances of a side-sleeping baby rolling onto his

Safe side-sleeping: Extend baby's underneath arm.

CARSEAT SAFETY

SIDS researchers have told me about many infants who died of SIDS in a carseat during a several-hour ride. Presumably this could be due to the "slumped" position in which baby's abdomen is pushed up against the chest and compromises breathing. Another possible factor is that the stomach outlet is pushed higher than the inlet, facilitating gastroesophageal reflux (see explanation of this condition, page 81) and consequent stop-breathing episodes. This tragedy can be prevented by observing the following precautions: During a long drive, frequently check on the breathing of your sleeping baby. Also, even though the recommended safest position for infants is in the center of the backseat, in my experience the danger of the driver taking his or her eyes off the road to check on the baby in the backseat may override the safer backseat placement. For this reason, many parents feel it's safer to put carseated babies next to them in the front seat. A recent innovation in carseat technology (for example, the Smart Move carseat by Century Products) allows baby to be positioned in a more reclining and less bent position, yet the seat will instantly switch to a more upright position in case of a collision. These carseat precautions are especially important for premature babies and other tiny infants who have exhibited breathing problems.

tummy, stretch his underneath arm forward. This arm can act as a stabilizer to keep baby from rolling onto his tummy. If the baby's arm stays closely tucked into his side, it will be easier for him to roll onto his tummy. Wedges to keep baby sleeping on his side are helpful, but *never use just a back wedge.* Rolling up a towel as a wedge between baby's back and the bed may encourage baby to roll from side to stomach rather than from side to back. Be sure not to use props that totally restrain the infant's movement. Freedom of breathing implies freedom to adjust body position as needed. I'm concerned that the multitude of commercial baby wedges may be more restrictive than necessary, and they have not been proven either safe or effective. For these reasons, SIDS organizations and researchers do not endorse these products. If you choose to use a wedge for baby's side-sleeping, it seems the most sensible to use a *front wedge only,* which allows baby to roll onto his back if desired.

If your baby is experiencing increased drool associated with teething, or mucus from a respiratory infection, the side position may help him handle it. The excess mucus is likely to collect in the lower cheek pocket or run out of the mouth rather than puddle in the back of the throat, as may occur when baby is sleeping on his back. So, if your back-sleeping teether is having difficulty clearing the mucus (evidenced by coughing, noisy breathing, and night-waking), try the side position.

Don't overbundle. It's best not to restrain baby's upper extremities. This always allows baby to adjust himself to the safest position for breathing.

It is unlikely that the warning against front-sleeping is just a passing fad. In view of what we know at this time, prudent parents should avoid placing their babies in the tummy-sleeping position for at least the first six months.[18, 19, 48, 51, 52, 57, 60, 61, 83, 158, 160, 170, 181, 216, 238]

7

Step Four: Breastfeed Your Baby

A nything that improves the overall health of a baby and sensitivity of its mother should lower the risk of SIDS. In both of these categories, breastfeeding shines. Here's how.

BREASTFEEDING REDUCES THE RISK OF SIDS — THE EVIDENCE

New research is confirming what I have long suspected: *SIDS is lower in breastfed infants.* A study from New Zealand shows that SIDS was three times higher in babies who were not breastfed. The risk factor for SIDS from not breastfeeding was even higher than from maternal smoking.[160] When I visited New Zealand in 1985 to speak on the subject of how breastfeeding and sleeping with babies may reduce the risk of SIDS, I spoke with Dr. Shirley Tonkin, a prominent SIDS researcher in that country. She shared with me her belief that SIDS does occur less often in breastfed infants. Of the eighty-six babies she studied in 1970–72, all of whom had died of SIDS, only three were breastfed; and this occurred in a country with a particularly high incidence of breastfeeding. Even the large collaborative study of nearly eight hundred SIDS infants performed by the U.S. National Institute of Child Health and Human Development (NICHD) found that SIDS babies were breastfed significantly less often, and if breastfed were weaned earlier.[95] It is interesting that this study did not separate out partial from total breastfeeding, so that a mother who breastfed in any amount was included as a "yes" in the breastfeeding statistics. Undoubtedly, many of these "yes" mothers were combining breastfeeding with formula-feeding. I believe that total breastfeeding provides even greater protection against SIDS.

The authors of the NICHD study concluded that SIDS rates were higher in formula-fed infants even after correcting for other factors, such as socioeconomic status.[45, 95] They also concluded that breastfeeding was protective against respiratory and gastrointestinal infections, two factors that have been implicated in increasing the risk of SIDS. SIDS infants between two and eleven months of age showed more upper respiratory infections within two weeks prior to death if they had never been breastfed. Another important finding in this study was that 74 percent of Caucasian and 86 percent of African American infants who died of SIDS were mostly or only fed artificial baby milk (formula).[45] The researchers in this study concluded that infants who were never breastfed had two to three times greater risk of SIDS.

Even though statisticians have tried to separate the effects of breastfeeding from other maternal factors, and some researchers, such as those performing the NICHD study, "corrected" for these factors, a definite separation of factors is nearly impossible. A Copenhagen study showed that SIDS infants were more likely to be formula-fed or breastfed for a shorter period of time than other infants. These authors concluded, however, that differences in breastfeeding between SIDS cases and controls merely reflected other features that were associated with SIDS, particularly socioeconomic factors and maternal smoking. But recent data from one of the largest and most reputable SIDS studies, the previously cited Avon Project in England, also shows that SIDS is lower in breastfeeding infants, even after correcting for educational and other socioeconomic factors.[60] According to Dr. Fleming, the more the Avon study progressed, the more it became evident that the incidence of SIDS is lower among infants of breastfeeding mothers. They concluded that breastfeeding is second only to back-sleeping position as a protective factor against SIDS.[61] The Avon researchers feel that one of the reasons SIDS was lower in breastfeeding infants was that breastfeeding mothers, due to their higher educational level, were more likely to be informed about and follow the advice of the overall SIDS risk-reduction campaign. A breastfeeding mother is usually one who takes good prenatal care of herself, and therefore of her baby; she is unlikely to smoke prenatally or postnatally, and if she does, she is more likely to quit when pregnant; and she tends to sleep with her baby and wear her baby a lot in a baby sling — all factors that I believe also lower the risk of SIDS.

So whether it is the milk, the mother, or the method that is responsible for the lower SIDS risk in the breastfed infant is hard to tell. It's probably a combination of all of these. Because there are so many other parenting factors that play a part in affecting the SIDS rate, let's rely on our innate common sense, as did the writers of the Declaration of Independence when they drafted the words "We hold these Truths to be self-evident." The authors did not say "And we are going to try these Truths out until they can be proven by a double-blind controlled study and replicated by three different researchers." Breastfeeding matters. Experiments, experience, and common sense tell us that.

The Milk

There are hundreds of substances in human milk that aren't in artificial milk. These cannot be manufactured or bought; they can be made only by mother. Each year researchers discover new factors in human milk that are beneficial to baby. I suspect that researchers have only scratched the surface of what amazing factors exist in human milk. The following is what we know. What is even more intriguing is what we do not yet know about how human milk benefits human babies in general and how it lowers the risk of SIDS in particular.

It fights against infection. As discussed, respiratory and gastrointestinal infections contribute to the SIDS risk, and breastfeeding infants get fewer respiratory and gastrointestinal infections.[7, 8, 44, 101, 132, 231] Breastfeeding protects against RSV (respiratory syncytial virus) infections, and this virus has been implicated in causing inflammation of the lungs, which could contribute to SIDS.[49]

Between two and six months of age (which, you'll recall, is also the peak period of SIDS risk), a baby's immunity is lowest and the vulnerability to infection is highest. As discussed in Chapter 3, the newborn baby derives much of his immunity from his mother's antibodies while in the womb. After birth these antibodies gradually disappear. Meanwhile, baby is making his own antibodies, so that by age six to nine months he is more capable of defending himself against infection. Between two and six months, when the antibodies derived prenatally from mother are at low levels and baby has not yet made enough of his own, the immunity factors in breast milk fill in, taking over where the placenta left off and protecting the baby while his own immune system matures.

One of the ways in which breast milk protects the infection-vulnerable infant is through the *enteromammary immune system.*[9, 120] When mother is exposed to a new germ, glands in her intestine make infection-fighting cells specifically for this germ. These special cells travel through her bloodstream to her breasts, where they announce the presence of the enemy germ. The breast glands respond by manufacturing antibodies, which are delivered to the baby through the milk. Because she can make new antibodies better and more quickly than her tiny baby can, mother updates her baby's immunity with every feeding. Would it be presumptuous to call breast milk a SIDS vaccine? Read on.

*It builds better brains.** "Mother's Milk: Food for Smarter Kids." This was the headline in *USA Today* on February 2, 1992. While both experience and research have long suggested that breastfed babies are intellectually advantaged, the difference has usually been attributed more to the nurturing of the mother than to the type of milk. But new research suggests that it's human milk itself rather than (or in addition to) the process of breastfeeding (or the skills of the mother) that enhances brain

---

*Initially, I was critical of studies claiming an intellectual advantage from breastfeeding. Mothers who breastfeed tend to come from the higher socioeconomic groups and be better educated. These factors enhance intellectual development in children regardless of feeding method. I had the same reservations I did for the relationship between smoking and SIDS. Was it the smoke or the smoker? The milk or the mother? Similarly, mothers who are less likely to breastfeed are the ones most likely to have many of the other risk factors that contribute to SIDS. Yet analysis of the studies leads me to believe that while these are valid criticisms and the methodology of the studies is not perfect, most researchers have employed valid statistical methods to separate the effects of other variables from the effects of breastfeeding. Also, while it is true that the breastfeeding mother of the 1990s has a higher socioeconomic and educational profile (which goes along with a lower risk for having a SIDS baby), many of the studies claiming an intellectual advantage to breastfeeding were done between 1920 and 1970, when the educational and socioeconomic profile of breastfeeding and formula-feeding mothers was the reverse of what it is today.[136]

growth.[136, 137, 141, 145, 161, 217] Brain-building substances and elements called "growth factors" have recently been discovered in human milk. Researchers in England studied three hundred babies who were very premature and weighed less than four pounds, a group that is at high risk for SIDS. They divided their subjects into two groups: those who were fed their mother's milk and those who were not. Because of their prematurity, these infants received the milk *by tube* rather than directly from the mother's breasts, thereby separating the effects of the milk from the effects of the nurturing. Those premature babies who got their mother's milk during the first five or six weeks of life averaged 8.3 points higher on IQ tests at age seven and a half to eight years. Also significant in this study was that the more breast milk the babies had received, the better these children scored.[136, 137]

Why does human milk build better brains? Special nutrients in human milk that are not in artificial baby milks may be the answer. Human milk contains substances (such as cholesterol, linolenic acid, and taurine) that enhance the development of the central nervous system in several ways, the most convincing of which is that it provides vital nutrients for myelin, the insulating sheath around nerves that helps impulses travel faster. (Postmortem examinations have shown deficient myelination in the nerves around the respiratory control center in some infants who died of SIDS.[116, 117, 118] These areas show changes that could be the result of delayed development and/or oxygen deprivation.) So vital are these brain builders that if a mother's milk is short on these special nutrients, the mammary glands themselves make and deposit them into her milk. Although myelination continues well into early childhood, the greatest degree of myelination occurs during the first six months of life.[21]

It is kinder to tiny airways. Besides reducing respiratory infections that clog baby's air passages, breastfeeding also helps keep little airways open by not exposing them to the allergens in artificial milk. Stuffy noses and airways and recurrent respiratory-tract infections are frequent signs of allergies to artificial milk made from cow's milk or bean milk (such as soy). Breastfeeding helps breathing in two ways: by helping the part of the brain that controls breathing to mature, and by helping to keep tiny air passages open. It is also interesting to note that breastfeeding infants have higher blood levels of the hormone progesterone, and progesterone stimulates breathing. In sum, babies who get the best milk breathe best.

As a final perk, even if human milk goes down the wrong way and enters baby's lungs, it does not irritate the lungs as much as formula can. Human milk is not a foreign substance, unlike infant formula. Also, studies on experimental animals showed that the introduction of water or cow's milk into the upper trachea (the beginning of the airway) can lead to apnea. This did not occur when normal saline (a physiological solution similar to the infant's own blood) or the species' own milk was squirted into the trachea. These researchers concluded that aspiration of water or foreign milk may cause a stop-breathing episode in infants, a life-threatening episode that might not occur if mother's milk accidentally goes down the wrong way.[50]

It reduces reflux. Gastroesophageal reflux (GER) is less severe in breastfed infants[89, 173] than in infants fed artificial baby milk, probably due to the fact that human milk is emptied faster from the stomach. Since GER has been implicated in ALTEs, and ALTEs may be a forerunner of SIDS, reducing GER could also reduce SIDS. (See "GER and SIDS," page 81.)

It promotes safer sleep. Since, as I believe, SIDS is basically a sleep disorder or a deficiency of respiratory control during sleep, it follows that anything that might make sleep a safer state in which to breathe might also lower the risk of SIDS. This is exactly what breastfeeding does. Both experience and research show that breastfed babies sleep differently from bottle-fed ones.[53, 76] Breastfed babies tend to awaken more frequently to feed, both because human milk is digested more easily and more quickly than formula and because breastfeeding mothers tend to be more responsive to their baby's nighttime cues. For these reasons, breastfed babies are used to waking from sleep in response to a need for food. *Could this easy arousability also "teach" babies to arouse from sleep when they have a need for air?* I believe, as do many SIDS researchers, that SIDS is also a disorder of arousability. (For a discussion of SIDS and a lack of arousability, see page 37.) So, if the sleep of a breastfeeding baby is blessed with easier arousability, it may be a safer sleep. Nighttime breastfeeding infants show more REM sleep, called "sucking REM." Babies are more easily aroused during REM sleep, so it may be the safest sleep state, although not all sleep researchers agree with this conclusion. (For the protective effects of REM sleep, see page 106.) Furthermore, in studies of animals, early and abrupt weaning resulted in a prompt decrease in REM sleep, rather than the more gradual decrease in the percentage of REM sleep that occurs with natural weaning.[194] Could there be a message in this statistic — that weaning babies early from the breast could increase the risk of SIDS? The data from the NICHD collaborative study showed a higher incidence of SIDS in babies weaned early.[95]

It organizes baby. I believe that an important piece of the SIDS puzzle is that some babies at risk of SIDS have an overall "disorganized physiology." (See page 41 for a discussion of the physiological differences in SIDS babies.) Breastfeeding has a calming effect on a baby.[198] The harmony between a breastfeeding mother and her sucking infant has an organizing effect on baby's sleep/wake cycles, probably as a result of the cue- response sensitivity of the breastfeeding pair.[92]

The Mother

Not only does breast milk have protective qualities for baby, but breastfeeding also does good things for mother, which indirectly may reduce the risk of SIDS.

It increases mother's awareness. Breastfeeding is an exercise in baby-reading. It increases the sensitivity of a mother to any changes in her baby. The increased maternal hormones (primarily prolactin and oxytocin) that are stimulated by baby's sucking appear to provide a biological basis for the concept of mother's intuition. During my twenty-five years watching mothers and babies, I have been impressed by the increased sensitivity breast-feeding mothers have toward their babies. They're able to read subtle cues and changes in their infants. Cindy, a breastfeeding mother, told me: "I can tell when my baby has an ear infection by the way she sucks." (See Chapter 10 for how attachment parenting increases a mother's awareness.) Breastfeeding mothers tend to sleep with their babies, a nighttime parenting style that I believe decreases SIDS risk. A breastfeeding mother also sleeps differently from her formula-feeding friends. She may be more aware of changes in her baby even while they both are sleeping. (See "Sleeping with Babies Reduces the Risk of SIDS — the Evidence," page 102.)

Can formula-feeding mothers attain this high level of sensitivity to their babies? I suspect they can, especially if they practice the rest of the attachment-parenting package, such as sharing sleep and wearing their baby. Yet without the hormonal boost that breastfeeding provides, formula-feeding mothers have to work harder at developing this heightened awareness.

The Method

Besides the good stuff in breast milk and the act of breastfeeding itself with its increased "touch time," the way an infant breastfeeds may also lower the risk of SIDS.[25]

It improves breathing/swallowing coordination. Newborns have to learn to coordinate breathing and swallowing during feeding. For premature infants (those at highest risk for SIDS), this is a gradual learning process. Studies show that premature babies who breastfeed coordinate sucking, swallowing, and breathing more efficiently than do their bottle-feeding mates. Breastfeeders also tend to feed more frequently than their bottle-feeding friends, therefore getting more practice coordinating their swallowing and breathing. Since tiny infants tend to have weak points in muscle support of their upper airways, their breathing passages are narrower, especially during sleep. Any exercise of the mouth and throat muscle is helpful in keeping the airways open.

In full-term infants as well, breastfeeding helps keep tiny airways open by helping the jawbone and muscles of the upper airway develop better. Dental studies show that breastfeeding babies develop better alignment of the oral cavity. New Zealand researcher Shirley Tonkin told me she believes that breastfeeding infants are more likely to use their jaws and pharyngeal muscles in a sucking motion that enhances the development of muscles and bones and lips, all of which helps keep their airways open better than those of bottle-feeding babies. Dr. Tonkin, a pathologist, speculated that the different muscle action involved in bottle-feeding may contribute to the growth of larger tongues, thus further narrowing the already unstable airway of tiny infants.[221, 222, 223] Recent postmortem findings that SIDS babies have larger tongues lends support to Tonkin's theory.[25, 203] The more stable the airway to breathing, the lower the risk of SIDS.[221]

In the previous chapter I discussed how putting infants to sleep on their backs or sides rather than on their stomachs may lower the risk of SIDS. When my wife, Martha, breastfed our eight babies, she invariably put them to sleep on their backs or sides, believing that in this position the breastfeeding pair had easier access to nursing at night. Breastfeeding mothers I have interviewed, especially those who share a bed with their infant, most often place their babies on their sides facing the mother; alternatively, the infant often sleeps in the crook of mother's arm, necessitating a back or side position.

As we await the results of more research, we can continue to rely on common sense. The milk of each species is designed to ensure the best chances of survival for the young of that species. (Consider what happens if you put the wrong fuel into a car. Sooner or later it doesn't run right and its engine control systems fail.) I believe that someday in some laboratory a researcher will discover what savvy mothers have long suspected: There are nutrients in mother's milk that help keep new lives living. In the meantime, it is possible that any one of the protective effects of breastfeeding could lower the SIDS risk, even slightly. When you put together all the benefits of breastfeeding — the good stuff in breast milk, the special touch of breastfeeding, and the special actions of breast suckling — you have a compelling case that breastfeeding increases an infant's chances of health and well-being.

8

Step Five: Give Your Baby a Safe Sleeping Environment

Because SIDS occurs during sleep, most of my SIDS prevention program focuses on providing a safe sleeping environment (in addition to the safe sleeping position discussed in Chapter 6). Before I discuss the safety of various sleeping arrangements, I will restate my SIDS hypothesis:

I believe that in most cases SIDS is a sleep disorder, primarily a disorder of arousal and breathing control during sleep. All the elements of natural mothering, especially breastfeeding and sharing sleep, benefit the infant's breathing control and increase the mutual awareness between mother and infant so that their arousability is increased and the risk of SIDS decreased.

SLEEPING WITH BABIES REDUCES THE RISK OF SIDS — THE EVIDENCE

The parents' bed or the crib? Which place is more desirable? Which is more safe? This question is a popular talk show controversy and the subject of confusion and disagreement among healthcare providers. Based upon my own research, the research of others, twenty-five years of pediatric experience, and seventeen years of sleeping with our own babies, I have come to the conclusion that the safest place for babies to sleep is with their mothers. This is undoubtedly the most controversial part of this SIDS prevention program. Therefore, I will explain in detail how I arrived at this conclusion and present the research to back it up. There are seven considerations that support my sleep-sharing hypothesis.

1. FACTS OF SLEEP EVERY PARENT SHOULD KNOW — WHAT SLEEP RESEARCH TELLS US

In order to appreciate how sharing sleep might lower the risk of SIDS, it's necessary to understand some features of infant sleep.

Remember the developmental principle that babies do what they do because they need to. This is particularly true for sleep. Babies don't sleep like adults. They are not supposed to. Let's look first at how you sleep and then at how your baby sleeps in order to appreciate the difference.

How you sleep. After dressing or undressing for bed, most adults help themselves relax for sleep by performing various bedtime rituals: reading, listening to music, watching TV, or having sex. As you drift into sleep, your higher brain centers begin to rest, enabling you to enter the stage of deep sleep called "non-REM" (non–rapid eye movement — NREM), or deep sleep (also called "quiet sleep"). Your mind and body are quietest during this stage of sleep, and you are sleeping soundly. Your body is still, your breathing is shallow and regular, your muscles are loose, and you're really "zonked." After about an hour and a half in this quiet sleep stage, your brain begins to "wake up" and start working, which brings you out of your deep sleep and into light sleep or active sleep, called "rapid eye movement" or "REM" sleep. During this stage of sleep your eyes actually move under their lids as your brain exercises. You dream and stir, turn over, and may even adjust the covers without fully awakening. It is during this sleep stage that you may fully awaken to go to the bathroom, then return to bed and fall back into a deep sleep. These alternating cycles of light and deep sleep continue every couple hours throughout the night, so that a typical adult may spend an average of six hours in quiet sleep and two hours in active sleep. Thus, you do not sleep deeply all night, even though you may feel as though you do.

How babies enter sleep. You're rocking, walking, or nursing your baby, and her eyelids droop as she begins to nod off in your arms. Her eyes close completely, but her eyelids continue to flutter and her breathing is still irregular. Her hands and limbs are flexed, and she may startle, twitch, and show fleeting smiles, called "sleep grins." She may even continue a flutterlike sucking. Just as you bend over to deposit your "sleeping" baby in her crib so you can creep quietly away, she awakens and cries. That's because she wasn't fully asleep. She was still in the state of light sleep when you put her down. Now try your proven bedtime ritual again, but continue this ritual longer (about twenty more minutes). You will notice that baby's grimaces and twitches stop; her breathing becomes more regular and shallow, her muscles completely relax. Her fisted hands unfold and her arms and limbs dangle weightlessly. Martha and I call this the "limp-limb" sign of deep sleep. Baby is now in a deeper sleep, allowing you to put her down and sneak away, breathing a satisfying sigh of relief that baby is finally resting comfortably.

You have just learned lesson number one in nighttime parenting: *Babies need to be parented to sleep, not just put to sleep.* The reason is that while adults can usually go directly into the state of deep sleep, infants, in the early months, enter sleep through an initial period of light sleep. After twenty minutes or more they gradually enter deep sleep, from which they are not so easily aroused. As you probably know from experience, if you try to rush your baby to bed while she is still in the initial light sleep period, she will usually awaken. Many parents tell me: "My baby has to be fully asleep before I can put her down." In later months, some babies can enter deep sleep more quickly, bypassing the lengthy light sleep stage. Learn to recognize your baby's sleep stages. Wait until your baby is in a deep sleep stage before moving her from one sleeping place to another, such as from your bed to a crib or from carseat to bed or crib.

Babies have shorter sleep cycles than you do. Stand adoringly next to your sleeping baby and watch him sleep. About an hour after he goes to sleep, he begins to squirm, he tosses a bit, his eyelids flutter, his face muscles grimace, he breathes irregularly, and his muscles tighten. He is reentering the phase of light sleep. The time of moving from deep to light sleep is a vulnerable period during which many babies will awaken if any upsetting or uncomfortable stimulus, such as hunger, occurs. If the baby does not awaken, he will drift through this light sleep period over the next ten minutes, and descend back into deep sleep.

Another hour passes and baby reenters light sleep, another vulnerable period occurs, and perhaps he wakes again, and so on. Because babies have such short sleep cycles, they tend to waken twice as often as adults, sometimes every hour. Furthermore, some babies have difficulty getting back to sleep; they have trouble making the transition through the vulnerable period of waking and reentering deep sleep. Some "resettlers" or "self-soothers" can go through this vulnerable period without completely awakening, and if they do wake up, they can ease themselves back into deep sleep. Other babies need a helping hand, voice, or breast to resettle back into deep sleep.

Babies don't sleep as deeply as you do. Not only do babies take longer to go to sleep and have more frequent vulnerable periods for night-waking, they have twice as much active, or lighter, sleep as adults. At first glance, this hardly seems fair to parents tired from day-long baby care. Yet, if you consider the developmental principle that babies sleep the way they do — or don't — for a vital reason, it may be easier for you to understand your baby's nighttime needs and develop a nighttime parenting style that helps rather than harms your baby's natural sleep rhythms. Here's where I am at odds with modern sleep trainers who advise a variety of gadgets and techniques designed to help baby sleep more deeply through the night — for a price, and perhaps at a risk.

Babies sleep "smarter" than you do. Sleep researchers believe that light sleep helps the brain develop because, as mentioned, the brain doesn't rest during REM sleep; instead, it works. In fact, blood flow to the brain nearly doubles during REM sleep compared to during the deepest state of sleep.[194] *This increased blood flow is particularly evident in the area of the brain that automatically controls breathing.* During active sleep, the body also increases the manufacture of certain nerve proteins, the building blocks of the brain.

Learning is also thought to occur during the active stage of sleep. The brain may use this time to process information required while awake, storing what is beneficial to the individual and discarding what is not. Some sleep researchers believe that active sleep acts to *auto-stimulate* the developing brain, providing visual imagery that promotes mental development;[186] the lower brain centers fire off electrical impulses toward the higher brain centers, encouraging these higher brain centers to react and develop better. It is interesting to note that premature babies spend approximately 90 percent of their sleep time in active (REM) sleep, perhaps to help accelerate their brain growth.

Observation of sleep patterns at different stages of life lends support to the sleep-learning theory. The younger the human being, the greater the percentage of active sleep. The fetus may have nearly 100 percent active sleep; the premature baby 90 percent; the term infant 50 to 70 percent; the two-year-old 25 percent; and adolescents and adults around 20 percent. As you can see, the period of life when humans sleep the most and the brain is developing the most rapidly is also the time when they have the most active sleep. One day as I was explaining the theory that light sleep helps babies' brains develop, a tired mother of a wakeful infant chuckled and said, "If that's true, my baby's going to be very smart."

Active sleep protects babies. Suppose your baby slept like an adult, meaning predominantly deep sleep. Sounds wonderful! For you, perhaps, but not for baby. Suppose baby had a need for warmth, food, even unobstructed air, but because he was sleeping so deeply he didn't arouse to recognize and act on these needs. Baby's well-being could be threatened. It appears that babies come wired with sleep patterns that enable them to awaken in response to circumstances that threaten their well-being. I believe, and research supports, that frequent stages of active (REM) sleep serve the best physiologic interest of babies during the early months, when SIDS is most likely to occur.[11, 20, 22, 41, 81, 88, 100, 131, 167, 171, 176, 191, 213, 223, 239]

Babies change their sleep patterns frequently in the first two to three years of life, with critical changes at two to three months. As I discussed in Chapter 3, during the first months of life, active sleep exceeds quiet or deep sleep time. A reversal of this relationship is noted in 60 percent of infants at three months and 90 percent of infants at six months of age.[202] The peak risk period for SIDS coincides with the period between two and four months, when the infant shifts from light to deep sleep. As the amount of REM sleep is decreasing, so is the ability of the infant to arouse from sleep in response to a life-threatening event, such as forgetting to breathe. Some SIDS researchers speculate that infants at risk of SIDS may develop adultlike sleep patterns — sleeping soundly through the night — before their automatic wake-up call mechanism is mature, a sort of precocious puberty of sleep maturity.[210]

As you will recall, this two-to-four-month developmental window is also the time when the infant's breathing, controlled during sleep primarily by automatic reflex in the earlier months, shifts to the control of higher brain centers. The pathways by which a child's brain tells her lungs to breathe (when the oxygen level in the blood falls too low and/or the carbon dioxide level gets too high) may not be as reliable during this period.

Nearly all babies make it safely through this two-to-four-month period of risk. A few don't, and need outside help. The sleep-sharing environment helps these vulnerable infants make this breathing transition more safely.

Pulling all these bits of research together, it is possible to draw these conclusions: Even though babies at risk for SIDS usually appear perfectly healthy on the outside, many of them may have abnormalities in their cardiorespiratory control center that increase their risk of succumbing to SIDS. These infants at risk seem to have two basic breathing abnormalities: impaired chemoreceptor sensitivity, that is, they don't breathe when they need to; and an impaired arousal response to breathing problems, that is, they don't awaken and restart when their breathing stops. Normally, infants have a sort of internal wake-up call that automatically goes off when they need to arouse from sleep to breathe. This self-protective system may be defective in some infants. They temporarily need an outside source to influence their arousability. If this truly is the basic mechanism in many SIDS infants, is there something that you can do to lessen this risk? Fortunately, the answer is yes: *Sleep with your baby.*

2. SLEEPING WITH OUR OWN BABIES — WHAT WE LEARNED

Our first three babies were easy sleepers. We felt no need or desire to have them share our bed. Besides, I was then a new member of the medical profession, whose party line was that sleeping with babies was weird, even dangerous. Then along came our fourth child, Hayden, born in 1978, whose birth changed my life and my attitude about sleep. Were it not for Hayden, this book might never have been written. Hayden hated her crib. Finally one night, out of sheer exhaustion, rather than dutifully returning Hayden to her crib, my wife, Martha, nestled Hayden next to her in our bed. From that night on we all slept better. We slept happily together — so happily that we did it for four years, until the next baby was born!

Soon after we ventured into this "daring" sleeping arrangement, I consulted baby books for advice. Big mistake. They all preached the same old tired theme: Don't take your baby into your bed. Martha said, "I don't care what the books say, I'm tired and I need some sleep!" We initially had to get over all those worries and warnings about manipulation and terminal nighttime dependency. You're probably familiar with the long litany of "you'll-be-sorry" reasons. Well, we are not sorry; we're happy. Hayden opened up a whole wonderful nighttime world for us that we now want to share with you.

Sleeping with Hayden opened our hearts and minds to the fact that there are many nighttime parenting styles, and parents need to be sensible and use whatever gets all family members the best sleep. Over the next sixteen years we slept with five more of our

Sharing sleep increases the mutual awareness between mother and infant.

babies (one at a time), and at this writing we are in the process of easing our three-year-old, Lauren, from our bed into hers. We are making this transition with some mixed feelings. On the one hand, it's nice to have the bed to ourselves; on the other, we know this special nighttime connection will soon become just a memory from our parenting past.

Not an unusual custom. At first we thought we were doing something unusual, but then we discovered that many other parents sleep with their babies. They just don't tell their doctors or their mothers-in-law about it. In social settings, when the subject of sleep came up, we admitted that we slept with our babies. Other parents would secretly "confess" that they did too. Why should parents have to be so hush-hush about this nighttime parenting practice and feel they are doing something strange? Most parents throughout the world sleep with their infants. Why is this beautiful custom taboo in our society? How could a culture be so educated in other things, yet be so misguided in parenting styles?

THE EAR IS NEAR

Some mothers who choose to sleep with their babies for fear of SIDS confided in me that they felt safer sleeping with their infants knowing that if their babies made noise and needed help they would be right there. Other sleep-sharing mothers felt that even if their babies died of SIDS (and they can, even with sleep-sharing) without awakening them, at least they would have the comfort of knowing they had done their best. If their babies died in their cribs, a distance from the parents, the mothers would always wonder what might have happened had they been sleeping together.

There is in fact some scientific basis for these mothers' beliefs. Conventional thinking is that SIDS babies go to sleep and never wake up; they just quietly forget to take another breath. This picture may be psychologically correct, as a way of consoling parents, but it may not be scientifically correct. As a former associate ward chief of the newborn ward at Toronto's Hospital for Sick Children, the largest children's hospital in the world, I had the grim experience of watching ill infants die. They seldom just sleep away. Usually toward the end they *gasp* for air. I've also witnessed premature babies take a gasp after a long stop-breathing episode, and then begin rebreathing. Some researchers believe that a "gasping center" exists in the brain that is triggered by depressed respirations as a sort of last-ditch effort to restart breathing, and that the failure of this mechanism to restart breathing may be the terminal event in SIDS infants.[219] Research in experimental animals shows that in response to oxygen deprivation, the infant animal's gasp acts as a sort of auto-resuscitator that stimulates them to breathe again. If oxygen is given after the gasp, the animal resumes breathing. So, it seems that the terminal event may indeed be an audible "last gasp," a vital sound nature intends as a signal to others. It is possible that if a baby suffers an ALTE, he gasps both to stimulate himself to restart breathing and to arouse someone nearby to help.

Also, new research on infants who died while being monitored revealed that the hearts of some babies gradually slowed to a stop even before the babies stopped breathing. [111] So, in some infants, the "Sudden Infant Death Syndrome" may not be either *quiet* or *sudden*.

What to call it. Sleeping with your baby has various labels: The earthy term "family bed," while appealing to many, is a turn-off to people who imagine a pile of kids squeezed into a small bed with dad and the family dog perched precariously on the mattress edge. "Co-sleeping" sounds more like what adults do. "Bed-sharing" is the term frequently used in medical writings. I prefer the term "sleep-sharing" because, as you will learn, a baby shares more than just bed space. An infant and mother sleeping side by side share lots of interactions that are safe and healthy.

A mind-set more than a place to sleep. Sharing sleep involves more than a decision about where your baby sleeps. It is a mind-set, one in which parents are flexible enough to shift nighttime parenting styles as circumstances change. Every family goes through nocturnal juggling acts at different stages of children's development. Sharing sleep reflects an attitude of acceptance of your baby as a little person with big needs. Your infant trusts that you, his parents, will be continually available during the night, as you are during the day. Sharing sleep in our culture also requires that you trust your intuition about parenting your individual baby instead of unquestionably accepting the norms of American society. Accepting and respecting your baby's needs can help you recognize that you are not spoiling your baby or letting him manipulate you when you welcome him into your bed.

What I noticed. In the early years of sleeping with our babies I watched the sleep-sharing pair nestled next to me. I truly began to believe that a special connection occurs between the sleep-sharing pair that has to be good for baby. Is it brain waves, motion, or just something mysterious in the air that occurs between two people during nighttime touch? I couldn't help feeling there was something good and healthful about this arrangement. Specifically, I noticed these special connections:

• Martha and baby naturally slept on their sides, belly-to-belly facing each other. Even if they started out at a distance, baby would naturally gravitate toward Martha, their heads facing each other, a sort of breath away. Most of the sleep-sharing mothers I have interviewed spend most of their night naturally sleeping on their backs or sides (as do their babies), positions that give mother and baby easier access to each other for breastfeeding. Other observers have recently reported the prevalence of the face-to-face position during sleep-sharing.

When I noticed this face-to-face, almost nose-to-nose, position, I wondered if the respiratory gases from mother's nose might affect baby's breathing, and, as mentioned below, there is some experimental evidence to support this. Perhaps the face-to-face position allows mother's breath to stimulate baby's skin and therefore baby's breathing? I have noticed that when I direct my breathing onto our babies' faces — a sort of "magic breath" — they take a deep breath.

Could there be sensors in a baby's nose that detect mother's

A FEAR OF OVERLYING

Some parents worry about rolling over and smothering their babies. The good news is that even with millions of parents sleeping with their babies, this rarely happens (especially when parents take the precautions listed in "Safe Sleep-Sharing," on page 134). Overlying has in fact gotten an unfair reputation. There are many more crib accidents than sleep-sharing accidents.

The same subconscious awareness of boundaries that keeps you from rolling off the bed prevents you from rolling onto your baby. Mothers I have interviewed on the subject of sharing sleep are so physically and mentally aware of their baby's presence even while sleeping that they feel they would be extremely unlikely to roll over onto their babies. Even if they did, their babies would be likely to put up such a fuss that the mothers would awaken in an instant. Martha, a sixteen-year veteran of sleep-sharing, also believes that a breastfeeding mother usually has such full breasts at night that she is unlikely to roll over onto her chest without being awakened by pain; since breastfeeding, sleep-sharing mothers nearly always sleep facing their infants, they could not roll over onto their backs and smother their babies.

The bad news is that overlying does happen.[13, 140] The great majority of cases of proven overlying (most of the suspected cases were not proven) have been the result of some abnormal sleeping arrangement: too small a bed, too many people in too small a bed, parents under the influence of sleep-altering drugs, or unsafe sleeping surfaces.

If you enjoy sleeping with your baby and all of you are getting more sleep in this arrangement, don't let the fear of overlying discourage you from feeling secure with this time-honored custom.

breath, so that she is acting like a pacemaker or breathing stimulus? Researchers have discovered that the lining of the nose is rich in receptors that may affect breathing, though their exact function is unknown.[236] Perhaps some of these receptors are stimulated by mother's breath and/or smell, and thus affect baby's breathing; one of the main gases in an exhaled breath is carbon dioxide, which acts as a respiratory stimulant. Researchers have recently measured the exhaled air coming from the mother's nose while sleeping with her baby. They confirmed this logical suspicion that the closer mother's nose is, the higher the carbon dioxide concentration of the exhaled air; the concentration of carbon dioxide between the face-to-face pair is possibly just right to stimulate breathing.[162]

- As I watched the sleeping pair, I was intrigued by the harmony in their breathing. When Martha took a deep breath, baby took a deep breath. When I draped our tiny babies skin-to-skin over my chest, a touch I dubbed "the warm fuzzy," I noticed their breathing would synchronize with the rise and fall of my chest.

- The sleep-sharing pair is often, but not always, in sleep harmony with each other. Martha would often enter a light sleep a few seconds before our babies did. They would gravitate toward one another, and Martha, by some internal sensor, would turn toward baby and then nurse or touch her, and the pair would drift back to sleep, often without even awakening. Also, there seemed to be occasional simultaneous arousals when Martha or the baby would stir and the other would also move. After spending hours watching these sleeping beauties, I was certain that each member of the sleep-sharing pair affects the sleep patterns of the other. Yet I could only speculate about how. Perhaps the mutual arousals allow mother and baby to "practice" waking up in response to a life-threatening event. If SIDS is a defect in arousability from sleep, perhaps this practice helps baby's sleep arousability mature.

- Then there was the "reach-out-and-touch-someone" observation. The baby would extend an arm, touch Martha, take a deep breath and resettle.
- I was amazed by how much interaction went on between Martha and our babies when they shared sleep. One would wiggle, the other would wiggle. Martha, even without awakening, would reach out and touch the baby and he would move a bit in response to her touch. She would periodically semi-awaken to check on the baby, rearrange the covers, and then drift easily back to sleep. (Keeping a baby appropriately covered or changing nighttime temperatures is a proven SIDS risk-lowering factor. This and other nighttime checks on baby's well-being is easier while sharing sleep.) It seemed that baby and mother spent a lot of time during the night checking on the presence of each other. I did not miss the hours of sleep I gave up to study this fascinating relationship.
- Our son James, an avid sailor, offers a father's viewpoint on sleep-sharing sensitivity: "People often ask me how a sailor gets any sleep when ocean-racing solo. While sleeping, the lone sailor puts the boat on autopilot. Because the sailor is so in tune with his boat, if the wind shifts so that something is not quite right with the boat, the sailor will wake up."
- In essence, the sleep-sharing pair seemed to enjoy a *mutual awareness without a mutual disturbance.*

3. WHAT THE "EXPERTS" SAY

To gather information about a possible connection between SIDS risk reduction and sleep-sharing, I went to SIDS conferences and consulted SIDS researchers. Some were less than receptive to my ideas and dismissed them as just another of the many SIDS theories that come and go. I consulted scientific writings and found that researchers are just beginning to study this obvious connection. No one even knew how babies normally slept. Babies were studied in sleep laboratories, which is like "sleeping" in a hospital, yet data from these studies were presented as the norm, as how babies were supposed to sleep.

"But my doctor advises us not to sleep with our baby," many parents tell me. I tell them they are consulting the wrong "expert." Doctors have no training in where babies should sleep. If you ask a doctor where your baby should sleep, you will get a *personal opinion* based on the doctor's own preference or a *professional opinion* based on erroneous information the doctor has read in medical journals that publish the horror stories of overlying and suffocation arising from abnormal sleeping arrangements and drugged parents.[140]

Another bit of bad press about sharing sleep came from the New Zealand SIDS study that concluded bed-sharing increased the risk of SIDS; its authors publicly advised against this custom.[159] I have learned that when research conclusions and common sense don't agree, suspect faulty research. That's exactly what had prompted the bad advice. After public and professional scrutiny, the New Zealand researchers retracted their warning, because their data actually showed co-sleeping was dangerous only if parents smoked in bed with their babies (which common sense tells us would be dangerous).[158, 193] The researchers who reanalyzed the original co-sleeping data have concluded that co-sleeping actually *decreases the risk* of SIDS.[60] As new co-sleeping data finds its way into medical journals, you will find more professionals who are supportive of sharing sleep.

After much frustration I realized that I was consulting the wrong experts. The most valuable information lay untapped in the minds not of researchers but of mothers who slept with their babies. They are the most credible experts. As I mentioned in Chapter 1, over the past fifteen years I advised parents in my

SIDS RATES ARE LOWER IN
SLEEP-SHARING CULTURES

The incidence of SIDS is lowest in populations that tradition-ally share sleep, but the SIDS rate may increase in these pop-ulations as their cultural environment changes.[214, 215] For example, SIDS rates are low among Asian immigrants to the United States, but a recent California study showed that the longer these immigrants lived in the United States, the higher their rate of SIDS, which could be related to the adoption of a more detached parenting style.[77] In Hong Kong, where sleep-sharing is the norm, the SIDS rate is one-thirty-fifth that of the United States (.04 per thousand in Hong Kong versus 1.3 to 1.4 per thousand babies in the United States). This finding is significant, because the crowded living conditions and the low incidence of breastfeeding in Hong Kong (only 9 percent, 4 percent, and 2 percent at two, four, and six months, respectively) are factors that should increase the SIDS risk.[215] In Japan, where co-sleeping is also the norm, the SIDS rate is one-tenth that of the United States. Just how much a lower SIDS rate has to do with sleep-sharing and how much it is the result of the other factors is impossible to de-termine. Most babies in Asian countries are put to sleep on their backs, and on firm sleeping surfaces.[55] Also, Asian moth-ers seldom smoke during pregnancy or around their babies. Probably all of these factors contribute to the reduced SIDS risk.

practice to try sharing sleep with their babies, not only because I believed that was the safest arrangement, but also because I wanted to see how it worked and what effect it had on parents and babies. Also, while on the faculty of the University of Southern California School of Medicine, I was teaching pediatric residents about to enter practice. One piece of advice I always handed out was: "Surround yourself with wise parents — learn from them." I decided to practice what I preached in this new interest of mine.

Over the years I have listened to nighttime stories from hundreds of parents (see "What the Real Experts Say," page 126) and have been impressed by the reports from numerous parents of their nighttime sensitivity while sharing sleep. For many parents, there is no doubt that a mutual awareness occurs while sleeping with their baby. In fact, it was these stories that prompted me to develop my SIDS prevention hypothesis. And though purists will argue that this is only anecdotal evidence, I must admit I have grown to value the wisdom of an intuitive parent as much as the outcome of the most meticulous scientific study.

When I formulated my SIDS risk-reduction hypothesis (described on page 102) in the early 1980s and published it in 1985,[194] I recognized I was taking a risk to be the first to publish such a controversial theory about such a sensitive subject. Yet I strongly believed it was true and that some day it would be proven. Parents who read my sleep-sharing hypothesis in *Nighttime Parenting* were overwhelmingly accepting, because it made sense.[194] The response from the scientific community was less than excited. As a proud member of the medical profession (and at this writing we also have two sons in medical school and one in pre-med), I have always appreciated the need to balance a wise skepticism with a cautious openness to new ideas.

During the 1980s I wrote many magazine articles popularizing the beautiful custom of sharing sleep. By request, I made the rounds of all the talk shows to debate this "new" way of sleeping. Yet, because of the seriousness of the subject, I seldom mentioned the SIDS connection. I became known in TV circles as "that doctor who advises mothers to sleep with their babies." Oftentimes I felt ridiculous giving my seal of approval to what was in reality such a natural thing to do, sort of like reinventing the wheel and extolling its virtues. Had parents' intuition sunk so low that some strange man had to tell modern women that it was okay to sleep with their babies?

By the late eighties, I was convinced that my sleep-sharing hypothesis was right, so I set out to study it seriously. Also, by this time I had shaken up SIDS scientists to the extent that they were motivated to study it too. In the late eighties there was a worldwide surge in SIDS prevention research, and the scientific community was becoming more open to the parenting-style approach to preventing SIDS. In 1985 I shared this hypothesis with Tom Moran, then president of the SIDS Alliance. Eight years later Tom told me, "We used to consider you a maverick. Now we believe you're on to something." Then, in 1992, a new baby, Lauren, entered the Searses' bedroom laboratory. This blessing, plus the availability of the new computer-assisted microtechnology, gave us the opportunity to study the effects of sleep-sharing on our baby's breathing in a natural home environment, and as this was the first time anyone had studied sleep-sharing in a nonlaboratory setting, we were invited to present the results of our study at the International APNEA Conference in 1993.[197]

4. OUR EXPERIMENTS

We set up equipment* in our bedroom to study eight-week-old Lauren's breathing while she slept in two different arrangements: One night Lauren and Martha slept together in the same bed, as they were used to doing. The next night, Lauren slept in our bed,

---

*Our thanks to Naptime Monitoring Company for their technical assistance and loan of $80,000 worth of equipment.

and Martha slept in an adjacent room. Lauren was wired (see page 123) to a computer that recorded her electrocardiogram, her breathing movements, the airflow from her nose, and her blood oxygen. The instrumentation was painless and didn't appear to disturb her sleep. The equipment was designed to detect only Lauren's physiological changes during sleep; it did not pick up Martha's signals. Martha nursed Lauren down to sleep in both arrangements and sensitively responded to Lauren's nighttime needs. A technician and I observed and recorded the information. The data were analyzed by computer and interpreted by a pediatric pulmonologist who was "blind" to the situation, that is, he didn't know whether the data he was analyzing came from the shared-sleeping or the solo-sleeping arrangement.

Our study revealed that Lauren breathed better when sleeping next to Martha than when sleeping alone. Her breathing and her heart rate were more regular during shared sleep, and there were fewer "dips," low points in respiration and blood oxygen from stop-breathing episodes. On the night Lauren slept with Martha, there were no dips in her blood oxygen, but the other night, when she slept alone, there were 132 dips. The results were similar in a second infant, whose parents generously allowed us into their bedroom. We studied Lauren and the other infant again at five months. As expected, the physiological differences between shared and solo sleep were less pronounced at age five months than at age two months.

Certainly these studies would not stand up to scientific scrutiny, mainly because of the small sample. We didn't intend them to; it would be presumptuous to draw sweeping conclusions from studies on only two babies. We meant this only to be a pilot study. But what we did learn was that, with the availability of new microtechnology and in-home, nonintrusive monitoring, my belief about the protective effects of sharing sleep was a testable hypothesis. I hoped this preliminary study would stimulate other

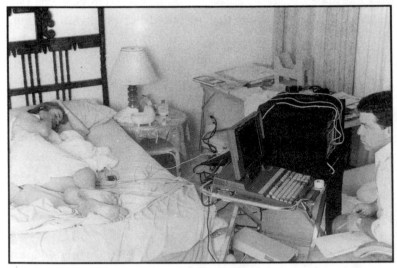

Martha and Lauren Sears sharing sleep.

SIDS researchers to study scientifically the physiological effects of sharing sleep in a natural home environment.

You may recall the story of Baby E.Z. from Chapter 1. Baby E.Z. was born at term but shortly after birth suffered respiratory distress requiring neonatal intensive care. A week after discharge from the hospital, a twenty-four-hour recording of her sleep and breathing patterns (called a "pneumogram") performed at home revealed frequent and long periods of irregular breathing and three episodes of apnea. Thereafter, the infant's breathing was monitored with an apnea monitor during sleep. The first two months on the monitor were relatively uneventful, with only one or two alarms weekly. The baby always self-started breathing within four or five beeps, by the time the parents reached the crib.

At three months of age the frequency and severity of the alarms increased. Between the third and fourth month, the alarm soundings averaged six a night. Early in the third month, Baby

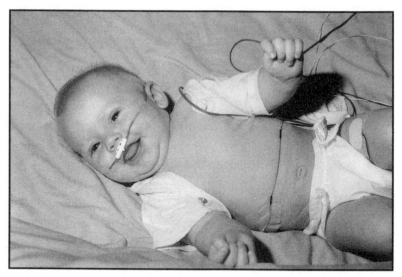

Lauren Sears wired for sleep study.

E.Z. would usually self-start breathing, but at age four months an increasing number of alarms required rubbing her back or bumping her crib to get her to breathe again.

On three occasions the patting and bumping did not stimulate her to breathe. On these occasions, her mother reported, "She was pale and grayish. I'd pick her up and she'd be completely limp, and it would take vigorous shaking and near shouting before she would be aroused and finally take a breath. On at least one occasion, I was just putting her down to begin CPR when she finally moved and breathed."

The mother went on, "Usually these alarms were only breath alarms, but occasionally, on bad nights, it would be the breath and the 'slow heart' alarm lights. We noticed she would go in cycles. She would sleep peacefully for a few hours and then begin periods of what we call 'bad breathing': shallow breathing causing several alarms to sound within a half hour or so. These occurred between twelve-thirty and one A.M. and then again between four and four-thirty A.M. The only way I could stop the bad-breathing pattern was to wake her up fully and then nurse her."

Baby E.Z.'s parents had become increasingly apprehensive and unable to sleep. When she reached four months old, I urged her parents to try sharing sleep, accompanied by unrestricted night nursing. I advised the mother and baby to sleep side by side, with the baby monitored as always.

From the very first night of sharing sleep and night nursing, Baby E.Z. never had a true alarm while sleeping with her mother. To exclude the possibility that Baby E.Z.'s apnea stopped only by coincidence or because of maturity, I advised mother to put the baby to bed in her crib as she had before. Each of the three times she tried the old method, the alarms sounded as before, whereupon baby was immediately taken into bed with mother and no further alarms occurred. After that, the parents reported, "How much better life is for all of us now that we're sleeping with our baby." The crib found its way to a garage sale, and the new sleeping and nursing arrangement went on for another year. Baby E.Z. grew up to be a healthy child.

WARNING: Parents whose infant is being electronically monitored should check with their doctor or monitor technician before sleeping in the same bed with their baby. It is possible that the older types of monitors may pick up *mother's* heartbeat and/or breathing instead of baby's, and therefore the baby may not be safely monitored. This is especially possible if mother sleeps in skin-to-skin contact with baby. The newer event-recording monitors are unlikely to be affected by the bed-sharing adult.

5. CURRENT SLEEP-SHARING RESEARCH

At this writing, the physiological effects of sleep-sharing are finally being studied in sleep laboratories that are set up to mimic, as much as possible, the home bedroom. Over the past few years, nearly a million dollars of government research money has been devoted to sleep-sharing research. These studies have all been done on mothers and infants ranging from two to five months in age. Here are the preliminary findings through 1994, based on mother-infant pairs studied in the sleep-sharing versus the solitary-sleeping arrangements:[53, 153, 162]

1. Sleep-sharing pairs showed more synchronous arousals than when sleeping separately. When one member of the pair stirred, coughed, or changed sleeping stages, the other member also changed, often without awakening.
2. Each member of the pair tended to often, but not always, be in the *same stage* of sleep for longer periods if they slept together.
3. Sleep-sharing babies spent less time in each cycle of deep sleep. Lest mothers worry they will get less deep sleep, preliminary studies showed that sleep-sharing mothers didn't get less total deep sleep.
4. Sleep-sharing infants aroused more often and spent more time breastfeeding than did solitary sleepers. Yet, the sleep-sharing mothers did not report awakening more frequently.
5. Sleep-sharing infants tended to sleep more often on their backs or sides and less often on their tummies, a factor itself that could lower the SIDS risk.
6. A lot of mutual touch and interaction occurs between the sleep-sharers. What one does affects the nighttime behavior of the other.

Sleep-sharing research is in its infancy, and the results of these studies are too preliminary to draw definite conclusions on SIDS risk reduction. Yet it seems evident that shared-sleepers sleep differently than solo sleepers. Whether or not this difference is protective remains to be proven. I believe it is.

At the 1994 National SIDS Conference, I had the opportunity to speak with internationally renowned SIDS researcher Dr. Peter Fleming. His initial conclusion from the Avon Project was that co-sleeping was not a factor in SIDS risk reduction. However, based on newer analysis of this study, he has changed his belief, stating, "Co-sleeping does seem to be an important factor in reducing the risk of SIDS."[60]

The next step in scientifically valid sleep-sharing research is to graduate from the sleep laboratory into the home, which we have shown can be done (see page 120). I urge SIDS researchers toward such home studies, as I believe therein lie clues to unraveling the mystery of why SIDS occurs during sleep. It is likely that within a few years scientists will validate what insightful mothers have long known: Something good and healthful occurs when mothers and babies share sleep.

6. WHAT THE REAL EXPERTS SAY

I have selected the following quotes from my gallery of testimonies from my "consultants." These are professional mothers who have lots of intuition. Many are also pediatric nurses. These savvy women know babies.

- "During the first six months of Leah's life, I noticed some dramatic differences in her sleeping when I wasn't sleeping next to her. In the morning I would get up while she was still sleeping. Since I had the monitor on, I would hear her loud, irregular, and deep sleep noises instead of the quiet, regular, light sleeping noises I knew. There was a definite change in breathing patterns after I got out of bed. I think that with her sleeping next to me, I actually helped her breathe. Maybe I was her pacemaker. I also noticed that by five months of age she would roll over onto her belly when sleeping alone. I never caught her on her belly when I slept next to her. She was always on her side or back."

- "When my baby slept with me I noticed there were times when he would stop breathing. I would wait, and wait, and wait . . . and no breath would come. When I decided I had waited long enough, I would take a deep breath myself. At that very instant, so would Zach! Hearing my breathing actually stimulated his own breathing impulses."

- "Our newborn was on a monitor and slept in a cradle next to our bed. I heard her gasping. I know baby noises, and these weren't normal. As soon as I picked her up and put her sleeping next to me, she breathed regularly, no more gasping. My pediatrician told me I was just a nervous mother. If her breathing didn't wake her up, it wasn't a problem. He told me it was my problem, and if I would move her out I wouldn't hear her. I kept badgering pediatricians to study her and indeed they found she had apnea 18 percent of the time. When she slept with me I noticed a difference until around seven months of age. She breathed with me. My doctor still thought I was a nervous, crazy woman, and he said my baby would be just fine if I would just leave her alone."

- "When my baby was three months old I went back to work part-time in the evenings. She became fussy and cried most of the time I was gone. By the time she went to sleep, she had worked herself into such a hysterical state that she cried herself to sleep. I feel that messed up her breathing. I would come home from work and put my ear down next to her crib, and I couldn't hear her breathing. Every seven or eight

THE VITAL ROLES A SLEEP-SHARING MOTHER PLAYS

From the research that suggests that infants at risk of SIDS have a diminished arousal response during sleep, it follows that anything that increases the infant's arousability from sleep or the mother's awareness of her infant during sleep may decrease the risk of SIDS. That's exactly what sleeping with your baby can do.

Mother acts as pacemaker. A major part of my sleep-sharing hypothesis is that mother can act as a breathing pacemaker for her baby. New research suggests that nearby sound can stimulate an infant's respiration during sleep.[211] Picture what happens when mother and baby sleep side by side. Together they develop what we call "sleep harmony." Both members of the sleeping pair have simultaneous sleep stages, perhaps not perfectly attuned and not all night long, but close enough that they are mutually aware of each other's presence without disturbing each other's sleep. Because of this mutual sensitivity, as baby normally cycles from deep sleep into light sleep, the presence of the mother raises baby's arousability and awareness. As previously discussed, the lack of arousability or ascending out of deep sleep may characterize infants at risk for SIDS. Countless times a mother has said to me, "I automatically awaken just before my baby starts to stir and I nurse her back to sleep. Usually neither of us fully awakens, and we both quickly drift back to sleep."

While watching Martha sleep next to our babies, I noticed how frequently she would attend to our infant's nighttime needs, often without even waking up. Several times throughout the night, she would adjust baby's covers, nurse, or do whatever seemed good for baby's well-being.

This sleeping arrangement does not imply that a mother should think of herself as a lifeguard, keeping watch every sleeping hour, day and night, for six months or feel that she is an inadequate parent if she chooses not to do so. This attitude puts fear into and takes the joy out of nighttime parenting. I'm simply talking about forgetting cultural norms and doing what comes naturally. Don't feel that you must never let your baby sleep alone or that you must go to bed early with baby every night. Remember that SIDS is a relatively uncommon occurrence, not a nightly threat to your baby's life.

Mother fills in a missing ingredient. In the early months, much of a baby's night is spent in active sleep — the state in which babies are most easily aroused. As I discussed previously, this state may "protect" the infant against stop-breathing episodes. From one to six months, the time of primary concern about SIDS, the percentage of active sleep decreases, and quiet, or deeper, sleep increases. More deep sleep means that babies start to sleep through the night. That's the good news. The concern, however, is that as baby learns to sleep deeper, it is more difficult for him to arouse when there is an apnea episode, and the risk of SIDS increases. By six months, the baby's cardiopulmonary regulating system has matured enough that the breathing centers in the brain are better able to restart breathing, even in deep sleep. But there is a *vulnerable period* between one and six months, when the sleep is deepening, yet the compensatory mechanisms are not yet mature. During the time baby is at risk, mother fills in. In fact, mother sleeps like a baby until the baby is mature enough to sleep like an adult. That warm body next to baby acts as a breathing pacemaker *sort of reminding baby to breathe,* until the baby's self-start mechanisms can handle the job on their own.

seconds she would take one or two gasps, and that's all I could hear. As soon as I picked her up and lay down with her on my bed, she started breathing more calmly and regularly again. She continued this panicky breathing in her crib at night for about a month. After that, I quit work and slept with her each night. That was my husband's idea. My friends had told me to let her cry it out, that she had to learn to sleep by herself. The panicky breathing that I heard when she slept alone in the crib was not the sleep that I wanted her to learn."

• "My baby had a cold for a couple of weeks and one night she woke up in her crib gasping and struggling to breathe. Her breathing seemed obstructed, but after ten minutes she was fine. I took her to the doctor the next day, and he reassured me, 'There's never a warning sign of SIDS. There is never a precursor.' I wondered, Is that because most babies are in cribs and so no one witnesses the warning signs?"

• "My baby had a breathing problem at night and seizures that were diagnosed as Sandifers syndrome with reflux and a seizure disorder. The sleep study at one university hospital was done while baby was sleeping in a crib alone, and it showed irregular breathing. I told the doctor that the baby normally sleeps with me, but he said it would make no difference and wanted to treat the baby with medication and put her on a monitor. She was now four months of age. I got a second opinion at another university hospital, where I asked them to do the study while she slept with me. It showed normal, and the doctors advised me to do nothing and stop the monitor."

- "Our baby would breathe like a choo-choo train when sleeping alone. When I would go over and touch him, he would breathe normally. When I took him into our bed, he would breathe normally."

- "I don't want to sound psychic, but I know we are on the same brain wave when we sleep together. We seem to be in perfect nighttime harmony. He nurses at night and I don't even wake up. Because of this, my life is so much easier than with my first baby."

- "At first I thought sleeping with your baby was nuts. Then our ten-week-old infant was diagnosed with GER. I realized I couldn't let him cry at night. It would be dangerous because crying brings on his reflux. So I slept with him, and he cried less. Now I'm so used to his breathing pattern that I wake up shortly before he does or when he changes his breathing pattern."

- "Because we had two relatives who lost babies to SIDS, we monitored our first baby, and he slept with me. I recognized when his breathing rhythm changed. My husband and I woke up seconds before the monitor went off. I tapped and stroked him, and he breathed."

- "With my first baby, for fear of spoiling, I didn't let her sleep with me (now I know differently), but she slept within inches of me in a bassinet next to my bed. When she was three and a half months old, I transferred her to a crib in her own room. That night I awoke in the middle of the night with a panicky feeling that I had to get to her. I found her not breathing. I gave her a shake and she started breathing. Evaluation at a children's hospital showed that she had frequent periods of apnea, from ten to fifty a night, and we hadn't even been aware of this. Then she went on a monitor, and our life revolved around the monitor. I was still afraid to sleep with her in my bed, because at that time the monitors didn't have a disconnect alarm, and I was afraid I would disconnect the monitor and wouldn't hear it if she had an apnea period. On many nights the alarm would go off every ten minutes to every hour. When she was around four months of age, in desperation to get some sleep, I would sleep with her on my chest in a reclining chair. On those nights, we all slept better and there were no alarms. Even when we were sleeping separately, many times I would awaken immediately before the apnea alarm went off. I believe I had a connection to her. I felt a need to have her close to me. I think breastfeeding her and holding her a lot during the day helped give me that connection."

- "Our baby has asthma, and I notice that if he sleeps in our bed his breathing is more regular and not as fast as when he sleeps alone. My husband has found he can also affect Nathaniel's breathing by pulling him close into his own chest with a big 'bear hug cuddle' and doing deep, slow breathing as well. This has become part of our asthma plan. Not only has it helped Nathaniel have more restful nights and require less medication, but my husband and I have had more restful nights as well."

- "Each of our five children has slept in our bed until two and a half to three and a half years of age, when they chose to move out. I noticed that they all would sleep with their faces toward mine, but if I were to turn my face away from theirs, they'd awaken. I truly believe that babies and mothers breathe in synchrony, and when one stirs, so does the other. It always seems like I awaken with our babies, not after them. And I believe that this breathing connection is responsible for it."

- "I slept with all six of my babies, and I think their breathing was more regular when sleeping with me. When I watched them sleep in the crib, their breathing seemed more irregular."

- "Our sleep cycles seem to be in tune. I wake up a few seconds before she does."

- "We feel we have sharing sleep to thank for saving our daughter's life. During our childbirth classes our instructor mentioned, 'You might consider sharing sleep with your baby.' My husband and I looked at each other and said, 'That sounds liberal. No way, thank you. She will have her own bed in her own room.' One afternoon when our baby was twenty days old, the high winds in our house caused the door to her bedroom to slam loudly. I thought she'd be scared, so I quickly went in to check on her. I found her gray, ashen, limp, and not breathing. I felt she was gone — I'm a paramedic. I grabbed her and she started breathing, and she seemed all right. After studying several nights of monitor tracings, the doctors concluded she had numerous episodes of periodic breathing like a thirty-five-week premature baby.

  "Sort of on the sly, my doctor said, 'You might consider sleeping with her and nursing her at night while lying next to her. All my babies slept in my bed until they were twelve to fifteen months old, and I've heard that a mother's presence regulates a baby's heartbeat.' I then said to my husband, 'Between my childbirth instructor, my La Leche League leader, Dr. Sears's books, and now my pediatrician, maybe we should rethink this matter.'

  "She slept in our bed the next ten months, monitored only by me. To my knowledge, she never had any more breathing difficulties. When people would say, 'Oh, she sleeps with you?' and give me a putdown look, I would simply say, 'Our doctor says it's best because it helps her breathe regularly.' In my college classes, I get so angry when people equate sleeping with your baby with 'doing something different.' It's natural, like a mother holding a baby. I wish they wouldn't try to make it such a liberal thing. I can't express to you how strongly I feel it made a difference. Our next baby will sleep with us."

From the preceding evidence it seems that separate sleeping could be not only unnatural for all babies, but even dangerous for some. Put new research findings together with the intuition of wise parents and you wonder whether sleep-sharing could not only make a pyschological difference but also a physiological difference as well. Each year more and more studies are confirming what savvy parents have long suspected: sharing sleep is not only safe, but also healthy for their babies. Thus, I leave it to parents to consider the following: *If there were fewer cribs, would there be fewer crib deaths?*

7. SAFE SLEEPING HABITS EVERY PARENT SHOULD KNOW

No matter where you have your baby sleep, be sure to give your baby a safe sleeping environment.

Safe Sleep-Sharing

If you have decided to share sleep with your baby, and this arrangement is working for your family, observe these precautions:

DOS:

- Take precautions to prevent baby from rolling out of bed, even though it is unlikely when baby is sleeping next to mother. Like heat-seeking missiles, babies automatically gravitate toward a warm body. Yet, to be safe, place baby between mother and a guardrail or push the mattress flush against the wall and position baby between mother and the wall (see illustration, page 110). Guardrails enclosed with plastic mesh are safer than those with slats, which can entrap baby's limbs or head. Be sure the guardrail is *flush* against the mattress so there is no crevice that baby could sink into.

- Place baby adjacent to mother, rather than between mother and father. Mothers we have interviewed on the subject of sharing sleep feel they are so physically and mentally aware of their baby's presence even while sleeping that they would be extremely unlikely to roll over onto their babies. Some fathers, on the other hand, may not enjoy the same sensitivity to baby's presence while asleep, so it is possible they might roll over on or throw out an arm onto baby. After a few months of sleep sharing, most dads seem to develop a keen awareness of their baby's presence.

- Place baby on back or side.

- Use a large bed, preferably a king-size. A king-size bed may wind up being your most useful piece of "baby furniture." If you only have a cozy double bed, use the money that you would ordinarily spend on a fancy crib and other less necessary baby furniture and treat yourselves to a safe and comfortable king-size bed.

- Some parents and babies sleep better if baby is still in touching and hearing distance but not in the same bed. For them, the sidecar arrangement works well. Remove one side rail from your baby's crib and place the crib flush against the side of your bed. Use clamps to keep it from shifting. Adjust the crib mattress to the exact level of your mattress and be sure there is no crevice between baby's mattress and yours. Special tape to seal the mattresses together is available from baby product catalogues. Lock the crib rollers or remove the wheels.

DON'TS:

- Do not sleep with your baby if you are under the influence of any drug (such as alcohol or tranquilizing medications) that diminishes your sensitivity to your baby's presence. The chemicals in alcohol and drugs lessen your arousability from sleep.
- Use caution if:
  1. you are very obese or extremely large-breasted. Both increase the danger of smothering.
  2. you are exhausted from sleep deprivation.[34] This lessens your awareness of your baby and your arousability from sleep.
  3. you are breastfeeding a baby on a cushiony surface, such as a water bed or couch. An exhausted mother could fall asleep breastfeeding and roll over onto the baby.
  4. you are the babysitter. A babysitter's awareness and arousability is unlikely to be as acute as a mother's.
- Don't allow older siblings to sleep with a baby under nine months. Sleeping children do not have the same awareness of tiny babies as do parents, and a too small or too crowded bed space is an unsafe sleeping arrangement for a tiny baby.
- Don't fall asleep with a baby on a couch. It is particularly unsafe for a parent or older sibling to fall asleep on a couch with a tiny baby. Baby may get wedged between the back of the couch and the larger person's body, or baby's head may become buried in cushion crevices or soft cushions.
- Do not sleep with a baby on a free-floating, wavy water bed (those without internal baffles), as a sleeping infant's face can become trapped in the depression formed by the weight of the head and the body. A baby may also sink down too far in the crevice between the mattress and frame or alongside the parent. At the encouragement of the American Academy of Pediatrics (AAP), manufacturers have agreed to label water beds

SLEEPING THROUGH THE NIGHT

Mothers and infants who share sleep have different sleep/wake patterns than those who sleep separately. Both experience and experiments have shown that babies who sleep next to mother, especially if breastfeeding, usually awaken more frequently. Whether this is desirable or undesirable depends upon the mother's mind-set about nighttime parenting and the nighttime needs of the baby. In one study researchers compared sleep/wake patterns in infants of different nighttime parenting styles.[53] Group one mothers breastfed on cue during the day and night and slept with their babies. Group two breastfed their babies but tended to wean earlier and sleep separately. The third group neither breastfed nor slept with their babies. Babies who breastfed and shared sleep with their mothers awakened more frequently and slept shorter stretches at a time; those who breastfed but did not sleep with their mothers slept longer; and the babies who neither breastfed nor slept with their mothers slept the longest.

In this study, the nighttime parenting style of sharing sleep and night nursing delayed the age of "sleeping through the night" three months past the textbook norm for Western societies. It's debatable which of these groups should really be the norm. My guess is that babies who sleep alone are training themselves, before their time, to sleep too long and too deeply.

After all, the greatest risk of SIDS is between two and four months of age, which is also the time at which babies begin to sleep for a longer stretch of time (or at least some books advise they should) — four to five hours. Because of this coincidental timing, some parents are beginning to question the accepted norm of sleeping through the night by six months, and many of them delay sleep-training strategies until after that time. Many parents consider night-waking normal (and for some babies perhaps necessary) under six or seven months, but a disturbance thereafter.

While sleeping too deeply, too long, too easily may not be in the baby's best physiological interest, a constantly fragmented night's sleep also diminishes a parent's and baby's arousability from sleep — a factor itself that can add to the SIDS risk. Every family needs to develop its own nighttime parenting philosophy and arrangement that will give all family members the most restful sleep.

"unsafe for infants." "Waveless" water beds (those with internal baffles) or water beds that are filled to become as firm as a regular mattress may be safer for sharing sleep. As an added safety measure, baby could sleep on a firm sleep mat rolled out on top of the firm water bed. If you use a firm or "wave-less" water bed, be sure all the crevices between mattress and frame are filled.

- Do not fall asleep with a baby on a beanbag or similar "sinky" surface in which baby could suffocate.[113]
- Don't overheat or overbundle baby. Be particularly aware of overbundling if baby is sleeping with a parent. Warm bodies are an added heat source. (See Chapter 9 for a discussion of overbundling and signs of overheating.)
- Don't wear lingerie with string ties longer than 7 inches (17.5 centimeters). Ditto for dangling jewelry. Baby may get caught in these entrapments.
- Avoid pungent hair sprays, deodorants, and perfumes. Not only may these camouflage the natural maternal smells that

baby is used to and attracted to, but foreign odors may irritate and clog baby's tiny nasal passages. Reserve these enticements for sleeping alone with your spouse.

• If your baby is being electronically monitored, check with your doctor or monitor technician before sharing a bed with your baby (see page 124 for explanation).

Use common sense when sharing sleep. Anything that could cause you to sleep more soundly than usual or that alters your sleep patterns can affect your baby's safety. Nearly all of the highly suspected (but seldom proven) cases of fatal "overlying" I could find in the literature could have been avoided if parents had observed commonsense sleeping practices.

Safe Crib Sleeping

Most SIDS deaths occur in cribs; the older term for SIDS was "crib death" or "cot death." So, if your baby sleeps in a crib, one of the ways you can lower the risk of SIDS is to increase the safety of crib sleep. Follow these safety suggestions:*

---

*These safety precautions pertain only to safe sleeping to reduce the risk of SIDS. For more safety suggestions to reduce the likelihood of other crib accidents, a pamphlet on crib safety is available from the U.S. Consumer Product Safety Commission hotline: 1-800-638-2772. Crib safety information can also be obtained from the Juvenile Products Manufacturer's Association (JPMA). Send a self-addressed, stamped envelope to JPMA, 2 Greentree Center, Suite 225, P.O. Box 955, Marlton, NJ 08053. In Canada, a crib safety pamphlet is available from Consumer and Corporate Affairs, Department of Product Safety, 1410 Stanley Street, Montreal, Quebec H3A 1P8 (1-514-283-2825).

DOS:

- Look for a Consumer Product Safety Commission label or a Juvenile Products Manufacturer's Association (JPMA) label stating that the crib conforms to safety standards.
- Check the space between the bars of the crib rail. The bars should be no more than 2⅜ inches (6 centimeters) apart, so that your baby cannot get his head caught between them. The bars of cribs made prior to 1979 may have wider spacing that does not conform to these standards.
- Be sure the mattress fits the crib perfectly. An undersized mattress will leave a gap along the side or end of the crib where an infant's head can get caught, causing suffocation. To check the fit of a crib mattress, push it to one corner. There should be no more than a 1½-inch (4-centimeter) gap between it and the side or end of the crib. If you can fit more than two fingers between the mattress and the crib, the mattress is too small. Remember, the firmer the mattress, the safer. Beware of hand-me-down or secondhand cribs in which the mattress may be different from the one designed to fit the crib exactly.
- Frequently check the mattress support system by rattling the metal hangers and by pushing the mattress on top and then from the bottom. If the hanger support dislodges, it needs to be fixed or replaced. Be sure the four metal hangers supporting the mattress and support board are secured into their notches by safety clips.
- To prevent choking, check crib toys, mobiles, pacifiers, and clothing worn in the crib to make sure they have no strings longer than 7 inches (17.5 centimeters).
- Make sure crib bumpers fit snugly around the entire perimeter of the crib and are secured by at least six ties or snaps. To prevent your baby from chewing on the ties and becoming entangled in them, trim off excess length. Remove bumpers and

CAN BABIES SMOTHER UNDER THE COVERS?

The newborn is not as defenseless as we might think. A stomach-sleeping newborn can lift his head from side to side to keep his nose and mouth unobstructed. Some observers noticed that even one-day-old babies will struggle and protest audibly when their air passages are obstructed. Yet others suggest that infants two to three months of age may not arouse to uncover their noses as quickly as newborns. With these protective defenses in mind, parents do not have to hover over their babies like guardian angels. Still, parents should take the commonsense precautions discussed in this chapter.

New insights, however, question the belief that babies rarely suffocate.[242a] In 1995, the Consumer's Product Safety Commission investigators found that about 30 percent of the infants studied who died of "SIDS" between 1992 and 1993 were found with their mouths and noses covered by soft bedding. For safe sleep, it's what's under the head that counts.

toys from the crib as soon as the child begins to pull himself or herself up on the crib rails, because they can be used as steps for climbing over the rail.

- If your baby's crib is not in your bedroom or within hearing distance of every room in the house, put a portable monitor nearby.

DON'TS:

- Don't use loose-fitting plastic mattress covers or waterproof sheets that can wrap around a baby's head and cause suffocation.

BEWARE OF SLEEP TRAINERS

Ever since parenting books found their way into the nursery, sleep trainers have touted magic formulas promising to get babies to sleep through the night. Most are just the old cry-it-out method in disguise, and technology has also provided us with a variety of sleep-inducing gadgets designed to lull baby off to sleep alone in his crib. Oscillating cradles, crib vibrators that mimic a car ride, and teddy bears that "breathe" all promise to fill in for parents on night duty.

While sleep training may be necessary for some babies, for others it may be unrealistic, even risky. Be discerning about using someone else's technique to get *your* baby to sleep. Weigh these schemes on your inner-sensitivity scale before trying them with your baby. Keep in mind that despite many studies of sleeping infants, we still do not know what constitutes "normal" infant sleep. The norm for "sleeping through the night" (which, by the way, is defined in most studies as sleeping for a five-hour stretch) may not be the norm after all. Older studies were performed on infants sleeping *alone* and in sleep *laboratories,* not on babies sleeping under at-home conditions. Newer studies suggest that babies may normally awaken frequently.[53]

Especially in the first six months, avoid sleep trainers who advise you to let your baby "cry it out." Only you can know what "it" is and how to respond appropriately to your baby. Liana, the first SIDS baby in my practice, awakened frequently. Emily, her mother, responded intuitively to Liana and nursed her back to sleep. When Liana was four months of age, grandmother advised Emily that she was spoiling Liana and that she should let her cry it out. That night

Liana's cries went unanswered. While there is no scientific evidence that sleep training causes SIDS, the memory of my first SIDS patient has made me wary of the hard-line approach to getting babies to sleep through the night.

I doubt that training babies to sleep too deeply, too long, too soon, while convenient for parents, is really in babies' best biological interest. Sleep training done before their cardio-pulmonary control mechanisms are mature enough to handle prolonged deep sleep could be risky. Training a baby to fall asleep and stay asleep alone in his own room in his own crib may be the "modern" way, but for some infants sleeping lighter and for shorter stretches may be the safer way.

- Don't place breathing blockers in baby's crib (or baby's sleeping environment). These include anything that could obstruct baby's breathing passages or collect dust, which is an irritant that can lead to stuffy little noses. Breathing hazards include decorative pillows, fuzzy stuffed animals and toys, string-toys, tiny chokable toys, and straps or ties on bumper pads.
- Don't place the crib in an unsafe area in the room. It should not be near a heater, against a window, near any dangling cords from blinds or draperies, or close to any furniture that the infant could use to climb out of the crib. When the baby gets older, give some thought to what could happen if she did climb out. The crib should be placed so that your baby will not fall against any sharp object or become entrapped or possibly strangled between the crib and an adjacent wall or piece of furniture.
- Don't attach crib toys between the side rails or hang them over the crib after baby is old enough to push up on hands and knees (usually about five months).

Safe Solo Sleeping

Besides the above crib safety precautions, to increase your baby's chances of a safe night's sleep, observe these dos and don'ts:

DOS:

- Follow the crib and mattress safety guidelines on pages 139–143.
- Place baby to sleep on her back or side, whichever way she seems to sleep the best.
- Spread sheets and undersheets smoothly and tuck them in tightly beneath the mattress. This lessens the chance of wrinkles in the bedding that could obstruct baby's breathing. Oversheets and blankets should be large enough to allow firm tucking beneath the sides and lower edge of the mattress, but at the same time not so tight as to restrict baby's freedom of movement.
- Be particularly vigilant when traveling, since baby will be sleeping in an unfamiliar and potentially unsafe environment. Bring along a portable crib or a roll-out safe-sleeping mat. These are safer sleeping alternatives than soft adult mattresses, such as the ones used in sofa beds or rollaways in motels. If you are using a hotel-provided crib, do a safety check, as described on page 140.
- Be equally vigilant when putting baby to sleep in a carriage. Observe the same precautions. Place infant to sleep on back or side, and remove any potentially dangerous objects from the carriage.
- Keep baby's environment as fuzz-free as possible, especially if your baby is prone to respiratory allergies. Besides removing stuffed animals, avoid bedding that is likely to collect lint, such as deep-pile lambskins or fuzzy wool blankets. Hypoaller-

genic mattresses and mattress covers are available for allergy-prone infants.

DON'TS:

- Don't put infants under six months to sleep on their tummies, unless your doctor recommends it. (See reasons for, page 78.)
- Don't put baby to bed on a soft surface, such as a water bed, beanbag, adult foam mat, or any other squishy surface that could obstruct baby's breathing passages.
- Don't leave baby sleeping alone unwatched in a carriage. An older child may caringly, but unsafely, want to snuggle a teddy bear next to baby's head. Carriage mattresses tend to be less cared for than other bedding, and they tend to collect dust and other allergens. Clean them as needed. Carriages are a common site of smothering in babies, second only to cribs.
- Don't use deep-pile lambskins or other deep-pile (greater than 1¼ inches, or 3 centimeters) sleeping mats for any babies. These not only collect dust and other allergens but can obstruct baby's breathing passages, especially if they get wet from drool or spit-up. Lambskins made especially for babies are free of toxic chemicals used in tanning, are low-pile, 1 to 1¼ inches (2½ to 3 centimeters) deep, and are safe for back- or side-sleeping infants. Don't put baby to sleep facedown on a lambskin. (Information on safe lambskins can be obtained from: LAMBY, 305 Grover Street, Lynden, WA 98264, 1-800-669-0527.)
- Don't cover baby's head after the first day or two. This is a baby's primary path of normal body heat loss. Covering the head risks overheating the baby, which increases the risk of SIDS. (Very premature hospitalized babies often need their

TRUST YOURSELF

The following story illustrates how important it is for a mother to trust herself when it comes to where her baby should sleep: "I was afraid of SIDS, but I knew little about it. I had no idea it was the most common cause of death in the first year. Nevertheless, I did vaguely remember that keeping a baby close to its mother could regulate its heartbeat and breathing. So, naturally, I did the only thing I could do: I kept my dear baby beside me in my bed. It felt so right to snuggle with her. I knew I was providing warmth and comfort, food, and, possibly, breathing assistance. When she was a month of age, I began feeling a little neglected by my husband. People told me I was overattached to my baby. She needed some space. I should let her cry. I began to reconsider my mother and mother-in-law's advice. Perhaps I was doing my baby a disservice by not allowing her to cry out some of her tension. Perhaps she did need some space by herself. I certainly needed some time with my husband. So, on that terrible night when she died, I decided, after feeding her, to put her down on her tummy in the nursery, but she wouldn't settle. I let her cry it out, thinking I would go back in a few minutes, but I drifted off to sleep to the sounds of her cries. The next thing I knew it was 2:00 A.M. I woke up with a start. Where had the time gone? Were the grandmothers right? Had she fallen asleep better on her own? Then I went in to check on her and to bring her back to bed to nurse. That's when my nightmare turned into a reality. I could not believe my eyes. My beautiful, healthy daughter was dead. You can imagine my thoughts. I felt I had abandoned her. Why, oh, why, did I listen to other people's advice and not to my own heart? There is such agony in doing your very best to care for your loved one, and then — without any warning, any sign — your baby is gone. What's worse, there is nothing you can do but blame yourself. But let me say, there is nothing more hollow sounding in the world than the statement 'There is no prediction and no prevention.'"

head covered to maintain their body temperature, but this will be monitored by the medical staff.)
• Never smoke in the room where the baby sleeps. Smoke irritates baby's sensitive breathing passages.

Observe these safe-sleeping practices, add your own common sense, and arrive at a sleeping arrangement that is safe for your baby and restful for your family.

CRYING IT OUT

The easy-to-give but hard-to-follow advice to let baby "cry it out" to sleep or "crying is good for the lungs" makes no physiological sense. Unresponded to, excessive crying can increase a baby's heart rate to dangerous levels (over 200) and decrease the oxygen level in baby's blood. Most babies can overcome this insult to their system. Perhaps some can't. [193a]

9

Step Six: Keep Baby's Bedroom Temperature Right

K eep your baby comfortably warm, but not too warm. Overbundling, and, consequently, overheating, have been shown
to increase the risk of SIDS.[63, 104, 160, 179]

The evidence. In two prospective studies, infants dying of
SIDS were statistically more likely to have been found in a
warmer room and/or more heavily wrapped than other infants.[60, 115, 179] Because of similar findings in a New Zealand
study, a 1989 SIDS prevention campaign in that country offered
parents a brochure titled "Keep Cool," with advice on appropriate bedding and clothing for babies. It also recommended the
back- or side-sleeping position. Within a year of this public information program, the SIDS rate decreased 50 percent in New
Zealand.

The reason. Overheating may disrupt the normal neurological
control of sleep and breathing. The respiratory control center in
the brain is affected by abnormal changes in temperature, and
SIDS researchers believe that overheating may cause respiratory
control centers in some babies to fail.[63, 75] Most infants are able to
keep their body temperatures normal while adjusting to changes
in environmental temperature. This process, called "thermoregu-

lation," allows the healthy baby to conserve and release just the right amount of heat to keep the body temperature right. If the environmental temperature is too warm, of course, infants sweat to lose heat; if it's too cold, infants shiver to conserve heat. But since tiny infants don't sweat or shiver as efficiently as do adults, they must also rely on parents to dress them appropriately.

The three-month-old infant (the peak age risk for SIDS) may not be able to handle excess heat as well as the newborn can due to several factors: As a baby grows from newborn to six months old, thermoregulation shifts from favoring heat loss to favoring heat conservation.[63, 64, 65] So, while newborns have a physiological tendency to get cold, three-month-olds have a greater tendency to get hot. As a baby grows from birth to three months, the infant's metabolic rate increases, which increases heat production. Meanwhile, the baby's internal body mass (the organs that produce heat) grows faster than the surface area (skin) of the baby, proportionally decreasing the amount of exposed surface for heat loss. In addition, the usual three-month-old is fatter than the newborn and thus has more insulation to conserve heat. The blood vessels in the skin of three-month-olds are also able to constrict better than those in newborns, giving them a further heat conservation advantage.

Another reason for implicating overheating in SIDS is the observation that SIDS occurs more frequently in the winter months, suggesting that something associated with cold temperatures increases the risk of SIDS. Studies in Australia suggest the single-most important factor influencing the incidence of SIDS is the climate. In southern Australia the SIDS rate is nearly ten times higher in cold months than in warm months.[17] This could be due to increased respiratory infections during cold weather, the use of central heating, warmer bedding and bed clothing, or possibly a combination of all of these factors. Perhaps this increased SIDS incidence is affected more by baby-wrapping practices than by cold weather itself. In Sweden, a cold-weather country that has low SIDS rates, most homes have central heating, and infants are bundled less at night. And SIDS rates are high in Tasmania, where fewer homes have central heating and babies are bundled more heavily at night.

It's important for parents to realize that current research suggests that a bit of overheating by itself is unlikely to cause SIDS. The reported cases were extremes: very overbundled babies, very hot rooms, often compounded by a fever-producing infection.

FIVE WAYS TO KEEP BABY'S TEMPERATURE RIGHT

Here are some practical things parents can do to help their baby maintain a healthy body temperature while sleeping.

1. Uncover baby's head.   Because the infant's head and face are the main source of heat release, it's important not to cover your baby's head. The environment around baby's head seems the most important for maintaining a safe body temperature. Baby's head is responsible for around 40 percent of the body's heat production and as much as 85 percent of the body's heat loss. This is why hospital nurses cover the head of a newly born baby, especially a premature infant. Note, however, that they remove the "ski cap" as soon as the preterm baby fattens and has a stable temperature. Covering the head of a newborn is sometimes healthful, but covering the head of a three-month-old may be harmful. Covering the head of an infant may cause a rise in brain temperature without a noticeable rise in body temperature, and the baby's respiratory control center may be affected by this overheating.

2. Put baby to sleep on her side or back.   When baby sleeps on her stomach (prone) with the full cheek and abdominal organs against the bedding, these prime areas of heat release are covered, thus conserving heat. So the phrase "prone to get hot" appears to have a physiological basis. When a baby is sleeping on her side, more heat-releasing areas are exposed, and sleeping on the back releases the most heat. Also, a prone-sleeping baby is more likely to slide her head under the covers and not protest at having her head covered; the baby sleeping on her back or side is likely to protest if her head becomes covered, because her face is more sensitive than the back of her head.[59]

3. Don't bundle up a sick baby.

Parents often tend to over-wrap sick babies, as if extra bundling were a part of extra nurturing. This is one of the instances where social customs and baby's basic physiology don't agree. Sick babies are likely to have fever, but when you cover a hot body, it becomes hotter. A mother may feel, "If I don't bundle her well, she'll catch cold." Baby already has a cold. Studies show that in the first three months of life, babies' metabolic rate during a respiratory infection either does not change or it decreases. For infants older than three months of age, the metabolic rate tends to increase with an infection. Thus infants older than three months of age (the age at highest risk of SIDS) respond to upper respiratory tract infections by conserving heat.[60] This biologic quirk may further increase the baby's risk of being overheated when sick, and overwrapping a baby with a respiratory infection piles one risk factor on top of another.[10, 69] As mentioned above, observers have also suggested that, paradoxically, the infant's sleeping room may be warmer in the winter time than it is in the summer, so that the risk of overheating is greater in the winter;[178, 180] researchers have also observed that babies dying of SIDS were more likely to be overwrapped than appropriately wrapped if they had been ill.

Dress a sick baby as you would yourself. When it's warm outside or your body is hot, you dress more lightly. During an illness, parents tend to overwrap babies when it's cold outside, even though the temperature of the baby's room is comfortably toasty. Be especially sensible about bundling sick babies for sleep. Don't overcompensate by overinsulating when it's cold outside.

4. Don't overheat the room where baby sleeps. Central heating may not be the most comfortable or the safest for sleeping babies. SIDS death-scene investigators sometimes notice an overheated room where the central heating has been left on all night.[65]

As a general guide, a sleeping environment temperature of around 68 degrees Fahrenheit (20 degrees Celsius) is preferable. Preterm infants or newborns weighing less than 8 pounds may require a temperature a few degrees higher. Healthy term newborns of more than 8 pounds usually have sufficient body fat and mature enough temperature-regulating mechanisms to allow them to sleep comfortably in a room temperature that you find comfortable.

Recent research has supported what grandmothers have always claimed, that if babies get cold, they catch a cold. The cooler the sleeping environment, the more likely babies are to get respiratory infections. Yet babies who are overheated have an increased risk of SIDS. In this study, the fewest respiratory infections occurred in bedroom temperatures around 68 degrees Fahrenheit (20 degrees Celsius).[64]

Consider humidity levels, too. Besides ensuring a safe sleeping temperature for baby, pay attention to the relative humidity in baby's room. Best is a humidity level around 60–70 percent. Less humidity may dry out a baby's breathing passages, making his nose stuffy and thickening the mucus in his airways. High humidity, on the other hand, favors the growth of respiratory allergens and may peel off the paint or wallpaper in older houses. As you might expect, most central heating is not friendly to breathing passages, because the air is either too dry or full of allergens. We have come up with a healthier alternative: Turn the central heating down or off during the night and turn on a *warm-mist vaporizer* in baby's room. (Because steam kills bacteria, it is healthier than cool mist.) This inexpensive steam producer (available at pharmacies and department stores for around ten dollars at this writing) provides two benefits: It increases the humidity in the room and it warms the room. From high school physics you know that when steam condenses, it releases heat. That's how the vaporizer warms the room. Don't let the humidity get so high or the room so hot that the paint or wallpaper begins to peel off or mold begins to grow. And, keep it out of baby's reach.

Be especially vigilant about bedroom temperature when traveling. Electric baseboard heaters, such as those typically found in ski chalets and motels, have a particularly drying effect on the air. It's worth taking along a warm-mist vaporizer or buying one locally. Except in extremely cold weather, a warm-mist vaporizer will keep a draftless motel-size bedroom comfortably and safely warm with the heater turned off.

5. Dress baby for safe and comfortable sleeping. Consider three things when dressing your baby for sleep: comfort, warmth, and safety. What style and fabric are most comfortable to your baby is a matter of observation. It won't take you long to figure out whether your baby sleeps better in footed sleepers or loose, tie-at-the-bottom "sacques." Learning how to dress your baby appropriately is really only a matter of common sense and getting a feel for your individual baby. Also, an appropriately clothed baby is more likely to reward you with a less disturbed night's sleep. Overheated infants tend to be more restless.[230]

As a general guide, dress and cover your infant in as much or as little clothing and blankets as you would put on yourself. Then, let your hands be a thermostat. Feel your baby's head or the back of her neck. If these areas feel too hot or if baby is sweating or her hair is damp, remove one layer. If baby feels cold, add a layer. In general, it's safer to adjust baby's sleeping temperature by changing clothes than by piling on more blankets. Baby's hands and feet are not accurate indicators of body temperature, since, in most babies, these parts are usually cooler than the rest of the body.

Consider these tips and precautions:

• Sleepers with feet are the most practical. Even if baby kicks off his blankets, you can be sure he has on one layer of warmth. A minor drawback to sleepers is that it's harder to get a good fit in a one-piece garment. Still, they don't need to fit perfectly. Buy them loose since they are quickly outgrown.

• Most of our babies seemed more comfortable (and had fewer irritating rashes) in cotton sleepwear, which absorbs moisture and "breathes," allowing air to circulate freely. Since cotton sleepwear allows for the release of body heat, it lessens the chance of baby becoming overheated. Flame-retardant cotton sleepwear is now available, yet it may be more difficult to find than sleepers made of polyester.

• Sleepwear should be loose-fitting enough to allow baby to move freely, yet snug enough to stay on.

• Leave baby's head uncovered, unless baby is less than 8 pounds and the room is very cold.

• For crib sleepers, use a single, porous blanket. Avoid heavy comforters, which don't "breathe." To keep baby from sliding under the covers, tuck in more tightly the portion of the covers beneath baby's feet or place baby so his feet touch the lower end of the crib. Tuck in the blanket snugly beneath each side of the crib mattress, yet don't fit the blanket so tightly as to restrict baby's freedom of movement.

• If you swaddle your baby, swaddle her safely. Experiment with different ways of wrapping your baby at bedtime. In the first couple months, some babies like to "sleep tight," securely swaddled in cotton baby blankets. Both experience and research have shown that swaddled newborns sleep longer, especially newborns who startle themselves by their random, jerky movements.[33] Swaddling contains these babies. But the recent publicity about overwrapping and overheating increasing the risk of SIDS may scare some parents away from the time-honored custom of swaddling. If your baby seems more comfortable and sleeps better swaddled, then swaddle without worry. Recent studies have shown that *safe* swaddling does not overheat babies.[80]

If you swaddle, be sure to place your baby to sleep on his side or back, and leave his head uncovered. If you swaddle your baby "burrito-style" (tucking each arm in the blanket and folding arms across the baby's chest) be sure not to place your baby prone, since he will not have the use of his arms to help him adjust the position of his face against the mattress. Arms-free swaddling is the safest. After the first month or two, many babies like to "sleep loose," and settle better in loose, sacque-like sleepwear that allows them more freedom of movement.

• Avoid dangling strings or ties on baby's sleepwear (and on your sleepwear as well). Remove any attached objects (decorative buttons, for example, or bows that could come untied) that might cause strangulation or choking.

• If you change baby's sleeping arrangement, change her sleepwear appropriately. For example, if you dress baby for sleeping in a crib in her own room and then take her into your bed after the first waking, consider the increased warmth baby may get sleeping next to you. (For additional information, see "Safe Sleep-Sharing," page 134.)

While overheating is a risk factor for SIDS, you don't have to become thermal engineers in order to get the temperature of baby's sleeping environment perfect. Babies are sturdy little persons with efficient temperature-regulating systems. If you use common sense and the above sleep-dressing suggestions, there is little risk of overinsulating your baby. In fact, under laboratory-controlled conditions, studies that compared usual night-dressing practices with ideal wrapping showed that 95 percent of mothers intuitively wrapped their babies correctly, so that their infants were able to maintain normal body temperature while sleeping.[3, 4, 114, 238]

10

Step Seven: Practice Attachment Parenting

The biggest breakthrough in SIDS risk reduction is the discovery that parenting practices can influence SIDS rates. A dramatic testimony to this change occurred in New Zealand, a country noted for its high SIDS rates and respected for the validity of its SIDS statistics. Following a national SIDS intervention program that discouraged front-sleeping and maternal smoking and encouraged breastfeeding and safe-sleeping practice, SIDS rates plummeted from 6.3 per thousand in 1979–1984 to 1.3 per thousand in 1990 — a whopping 80 percent reduction.

These groundbreaking findings are a wake-up call to SIDS researchers who cling to the conventional thinking that SIDS is a nonpreventable tragedy. While the nonpreventability of SIDS is still a popular and emotionally correct belief, in light of recent research, this concept is no longer scientifically correct. In the final step of this risk-reduction program I propose that an overall style of caregiving called "attachment parenting" will further reduce the risk of SIDS.

WHAT IS ATTACHMENT PARENTING?

In the early 1980s, after years of studying the effects of what parents do and how their children turn out, I coined the term "attachment parenting," and wrote about it in my first book, *Creative Parenting.* In 1985, in my book *Nighttime Parenting,* I described how this high-touch style of parenting could reduce the risk of SIDS.

Attachment parenting is a way of caring that helps mother and infant get connected, become mutually sensitive, and develop the skills that help them both thrive. With this parenting style, mother and baby, during at least the first six months, spend most, if not all, of their time in physical and emotional touch with each other. Attachment parenting builds a mother's relationship with her baby. Mother and baby become so attuned to one another that they enhance each other's behavior and physiology. Each is necessary to the other's sense of well-being.

Here's what mothers and fathers who practice this style of parenting have to say about what it does for their relationship with their baby:

- "I know her so well."
- "I can read him."
- "I've developed a sixth sense about my baby."
- "I'm so aware of her changing needs."
- "It's like ESP; I feel so tuned in to her needs."
- "I feel so connected to my baby."
- "Attachment parenting feels so natural to me. It just feels right."
- "It's comforting to really know what he needs."
- "I feel a radarlike awareness of my baby."

Here are the three main elements of attachment parenting:

1. breastfeeding your baby
2. sharing sleep with your baby
3. wearing your baby

In previous chapters I have already discussed how breastfeeding and sharing sleep with your baby can lower the risk of SIDS. Before showing how the overall style of attachment parenting can lower the risk of SIDS, I want to discuss how the third element of attachment, wearing your baby, can lower the risk.

BABYWEARING AND SIDS RISK REDUCTION

If SIDS is basically a disorder of respiratory control and neurological immaturity (as I believe it is), anything that can help a baby's neurological system mature overall will lower the risk of SIDS. That's exactly what babywearing does.*

While wearing our own babies, I noticed how my breathing affected theirs, especially when I was sitting still with a sleeping baby nestled in a sling against my chest. Whenever I took a deep breath, so did baby. Sometimes the stimulus was the rise and fall of my chest; at other times the air exhaled from my mouth and nose against baby's scalp or cheek stimulated baby to take a deep breath.

Have you ever wondered why mothers in other cultures have for centuries worn their babies in homemade slings? I used to believe this old custom's purpose was simply to protect babies from jungle dangers or to enable mothers to do manual labor, and that in civilized cultures it wasn't so necessary to wear babies. Wrong! When I was researching parenting styles in other cultures, I interviewed African mothers who wore their babies in slings that were extensions of their own clothing. They agreed that babywearing protected their infants from dangers, but that wasn't the main reason for doing it. Instead, they said, "It makes life easier

---

*See *The Baby Book* for a complete description of how to wear babies at different ages and in a variety of circumstances.[197]

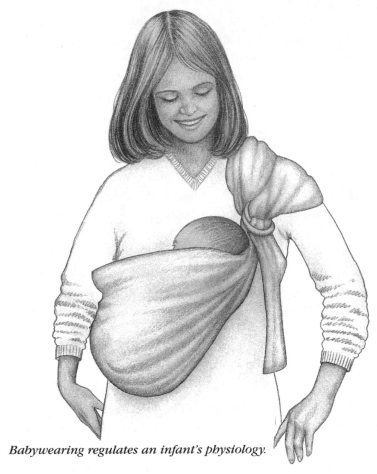

Babywearing regulates an infant's physiology.

for the mother," or "It does good things for the babies." "What good things?" I inquired. These mothers replied, "The babies seem happier," or "They cry less," or "They seem more content," or "The babies grow better." Note, these observations were not from mothers who attended parenting classes, read books on baby bonding, or relied on scientific studies. These were mothers whose "sources" were their own powers of keen observation and centuries of tradition, both of which told them babies thrive better when carried in slings. Now, modern researchers have scientifically proven what these intuitive mothers have long known: Something good happens to babies who spend a lot of time nestled close to nurturing caregivers.[12, 135, 220] Here's why.

The vestibular connection. Babywearing exerts a regulatory effect on the baby, primarily through the vestibular system. This tiny system, located behind each ear, controls baby's sense of internal balance. It is as if there are three tiny carpenter's levels back there, one tracking side-to-side motion, another for up-and-down motion, and a third for back-and-forth motion, all functioning together to keep the body in balance. Every time the baby moves, the fluid in these "levels" moves against tiny hairlike filaments that vibrate, which sends messages to the brain to help baby balance her body.

In the womb, the baby's very sensitive vestibular system is constantly stimulated, because a fetus experiences almost continuous motion. Babywearing provides the same kind of three-dimensional stimulation and "reminds" the baby of the motion and balance he enjoyed in the womb. The rhythm of the mother's walk, which baby got so used to in the womb, is experienced again in the "outside womb" during babywearing.

Activities such as rocking and carrying stimulate the baby's vestibular system. Vestibular stimulation is a recently appreciated tool for helping babies breathe and grow better, especially premature infants — those at highest risk of SIDS.[79] With the exception of one, studies done on premature babies placed on professionally monitored oscillating water beds showed that they grew better and had fewer apnea episodes than other preemies did.[124, 187] Babies themselves recognize that they need vestibular stimulation; infants deprived of adequate vestibular stimulation often attempt to put themselves into motion on their own, with less efficient movements, such as self-rocking. Researchers believe that vestibular stimulation has a regulating effect on an infant's overall physiology and motor development.[1]

Kangaroo care. Newborn nurseries have recently begun using a method of vestibular stimulation called "kangaroo care," in which a premature baby is wrapped, skin-to-skin, up against the mother's or father's chest. The parent rocks, holds, and gently moves with the baby. The rocking motion, the skin contact, and the rhythmic motion of the parent's chest during breathing produce the following beneficial physiological effects in the babies:

- more stable heart rates
- more even breathing
- fewer episodes of periodic breathing
- fewer and shorter episodes of apnea
- a healthier level of oxygen in their blood
- faster growth
- less crying and increased time in the state of quiet alertness
- better sleeping

Researchers believe that, using kangaroo care, the parent acts as a regulator of baby's physiology, including reminding the baby to breathe.[5, 92, 93, 138, 220] In other experiments, infants with breathing difficulties were placed next to a teddy bear stuffed with a mechanism that seemed to "breathe"; these babies also had fewer apnea episodes. When this "breakthrough" in teddy technology hit the newspapers, a reader wrote in, "Why not use the real mother?"

As an example of how closeness regulates a baby's breathing, a mother shared the following story with me: "My baby was born four weeks premature at five pounds, fifteen ounces. I held her all day long, never put her in the bassinet, and she breastfed well. She seemed perfectly healthy, pink, and breathed normally. That

ARE NEW WAYS THE SAFEST WAYS?

Could infants' biological needs and modern parenting practices be at odds? In the early 1900s, due to a variety of socioeconomic reasons, parents turned to a less connected parenting style, namely formula feeding and solo sleeping. Buggies replaced slings for transporting infants; bottles replaced breasts for feeding them. And, baby-book writers added to this parent-infant distancing by preaching scheduled feedings and warning against terminal dependency and marital discord if parents allowed their babies into their beds. Infant-care catalogs were filled with synthetic soothers that freed parents from the simple pleasures of holding their babies. "Infant independence" became the parenting dream.

Conventional thinking says that human infants should be able to adapt to the "norms" of the society they are raised in. But, do infants' biological needs and parents' expectations agree?[122] Consider this evidence:

• The nature of the milk of each species gives a clue to the style of parenting the offspring need.[197] Some mammals park their young for long periods while the parents are away hunting. The milk of these mammals is high in fat and calories to satisfy the infant for long periods. These mammals are what is called an "intermittent-contact species." Human milk, on the other hand, is relatively low in fat and calories, indicating nature intended human infants to be fed frequently. Human infants are a "constant-contact species." Anthropologists dub these two parenting styles "cache" (meaning infants are left alone for long periods) or "carry" (infants are worn in babyslings and nursed frequently).[135]

• A human infant is born with only 25 percent of its final brain growth, around half as mature as other mammals at birth. The human newborn is more neurologically dependent than other newborn mammals are.

Attachment parenting puts babies at a biological advantage to protect themselves; a more distant style of parenting could put babies at a disadvantage. Their brain, heart, and lungs are the systems most likely to fail in SIDS. Interestingly, these are the systems most benefited by attachment parenting. While it may be politically correct for modern infant-care advisors to preach "options" in parenting practices, pushing an infant into independence too soon may not be biologically correct. For some infants, it may even be risky.

True, the human infant is a sturdy little person, able to adapt to a wide variety of parenting practices, but perhaps one infant out of a thousand can't.

Attachment research suggests a change of mind-set in terms of how we view infants. Instead of regarding the infant as exiting from the womb and immediately being put on the fast track toward independence, perhaps we should be thinking along the lines of *interdependence* — meaning during the early months, mother and infant need to be in frequent contact with each other in order to bring out the best in each other.

evening when the pediatrician came to check her, she took her into the nursery and put her in the bassinet. As soon as our baby was lying in the bassinet alone she had stop-breathing episodes, which alarmed the neonatologists, and she was put into intensive care for nine days. They never did find out why she had apneic episodes, although they thought this was due to a 'slight seizure disorder.' All they had to do was touch her and she would start breathing again. She never had any stop-breathing episodes when she was in my arms, only when she was lying alone. The doctors told me she was a prime candidate for SIDS. They convinced me that she needed to be on a home infant monitor. I agreed, but that turned out to be a nightmare for our whole family. They told me not to put her into my bed, so she slept alone with the monitor. The monitor went off all night long, probably from false alarms, and no one got any sleep. I left her on the monitor but put her next to me and slept with her side by side. (See page 124 for precautions on sleeping with your baby on a monitor.) We both slept wonderfully, and the monitor alarm never sounded. I strongly feel that my presence stimulated her to breathe until she outgrew her stop-breathing tendencies. My touch and closeness to her was all she needed. In fact, while she was in my arms in the hospital all day long no one ever knew she had a 'breathing problem.' "

Motion regulates babies. Motion calms babies. Carried infants show a heightened level of *quiet alertness,* the behavioral state in which infants best interact with and learn from their environment.[123] Researchers believe that during the state of quiet alertness, the child's whole physiological system works better.[54]

Carried babies cry less. Parents in my practice commonly report, "As long as I wear her, she's content!" Parents of fussy babies who try babywearing relate that their babies seem to forget to fuss. This is more than just my own impression. In 1986, a team of pediatricians in Montreal reported on a study of ninety-nine mother-infant pairs, half of whom were assigned to a group that was asked to carry their babies for at least three extra hours a day and were provided with baby carriers.[12] The parents in this group were encouraged to carry their infants throughout the day regardless of the state of the infant, not just in response to crying or fussing, although the usual practice in Western society is to pick up and carry the baby mainly after the crying has started. In the control, or noncarried group, parents were not given any specific instructions about carrying. After six weeks, the infants who received supplemental carrying cried and fussed 43 percent less than the noncarried group.

Anthropologists who travel throughout the world studying infant-care practices in other cultures agree that infants in baby-wearing cultures cry much less. In Western culture we measure a baby's crying in hours per day, but in other cultures, crying is measured in minutes. We have been led to believe that it is "normal" for babies to cry a lot, but in other cultures this is not accepted as the norm. In these cultures, babies are normally "up" in arms and are put down only to sleep — next to the mother. When the parent must attend to her own needs, the baby is in someone else's arms.

In addition to the physiological effects of vestibular stimulation, there appear to be psychological benefits. Sling babies seem to show a feeling of rightness enabling them to adapt to all that is unfamiliar about the world to which they are now exposed, lessening their anxiety and need to fuss. As baby senses mother's rhythmic breathing while worn tummy to tummy, chest to chest, the babywearing mother acts as a regulator of her infant's biology.

HOW ATTACHMENT PARENTING CAN REDUCE THE RISK OF SIDS

As previously discussed, the most plausible explanation for SIDS, in most babies, is that there is a defect in cardiorespiratory control and arousability during sleep. Also, research suggests that some infants at risk for SIDS have less-organized physiological

Keeps stress hormones in balance.

Increases brain growth-promoting substances.

Enhances infant's body-heat regulation.

Promotes hormones that help baby *thrive*.

Improves energy efficiency of baby's overall physiology.

Promotes self-protective sleep patterns.

Improves function of the three systems implicated in SIDS: brain, heart, and lungs.

Enhances maternal hormones that increase the awareness and sensitivity between mother and infant.

Enhances infant's immunity to infection.

To: My baby

Physiological benefits of attachment parenting.

THE NEED-LEVEL CONCEPT

During my years as a mother-and-baby–watcher, I've observed something I call the "need-level concept." I believe that every baby has a certain level of need that must be filled if that baby is to thrive. Fortunately, most infants also come wired with a corresponding temperament that lets their parents know the level of care they need. For example, babies who have a high need to be held will protest if they are put down. A baby who needs a high level of nighttime touch will protest sleeping alone. When the need level of the infant and the giving level of the parents match, this baby feels that he *fits* — a tiny word that economically describes a feeling of rightness (both emotional and physiological) that an attachment-parented baby has. Perhaps an infant at highest risk of SIDS is also the neediest of a full dose of attachment parenting: breastfeeding, sharing sleep, and babywearing. Another infant may need only one or two of these attachment tools to boost her physiology to the level she needs to thrive. A high-need baby who receives a more distant style of parenting may have a physiology that functions with a very narrow margin of safety. Give that baby a full course of attachment parenting, and that infant gets a biological boost during the risky period of SIDS. *For high-need babies, it helps to think of the womb lasting eighteen months, nine months of attachment inside and nine more months of attachment outside.* Infants whose need levels are not met may fuss more to pester the parents to upgrade their style of care — witness the parent who says "As long as I carry him he's content." Or, consider the

> high-need baby in "easy baby" disguise who really needs a full dose of attachment parenting but doesn't have the demanding temperament to get it. Also, there is the infant who, instead of fussing to get picked up, gives up, becomes apathetic, and withdraws — a reaction I call "the shutdown syndrome."

control mechanisms. So, any parenting style that can enhance the development of a baby's physiological control systems and increase mother's awareness to subtle changes in her baby's physiology would lower the risk of SIDS. Attachment parenting does this.

Attachment parenting organizes an infant's physiological control systems. New thinking is that some SIDS babies may not have been as physiologically normal as they appeared to be before they died. Findings of higher heart rates and less-adaptable heart-rate variability in babies at risk for SIDS suggests these infants are less able to adjust their physiology to changing biological conditions. Also, several studies of high-risk infants and babies who died of SIDS suggests that some of these babies had temperaments and behavioral qualities that lessened their ability to protest life-threatening circumstances. Summing up this complicated and shaky research that attempts to correlate infant temperament and SIDS, it seems that in some infants the *drive to survive* is weak.[30] Some infants are physiologically disadvantaged to protect themselves from SIDS. The results of fascinating studies on psychobiology (the relationship between how babies feel emotionally and how well their physiology performs) often never reach the general public.

A baby who spends a lot of time in mother's arms, at mother's breasts, and in mother's bed becomes more *physiologically organized.* Therefore, I believe a baby whose overall physiology is more organized has a lower risk of succumbing to SIDS. "Pure speculation," researchers would claim! Read on. Over a period of fifteen years I have gathered hundreds of articles on attachment research, studies that conclude the closer the infant and mother are, the better the baby's physiology works, especially during the early months, when infants are at highest risk of SIDS. What a pity that most of this useful research lies buried in obscure journals or is shared only at scientific meetings, with little translated into practical information to help new parents develop a style of infant care that could reduce the risk of SIDS.

Circulating throughout the bloodstream of every person, even tiny babies, is an adrenal hormone called "cortisol." Produced by the adrenal glands, this hormone helps major systems of the body function normally. The body needs just the right amount of cortisol at the right times. Too much or too little, and the body is not in tune, sort of like an engine trying to run with the wrong mix of gasoline and air. Adrenal hormones are also known as stress hormones. Levels rise quickly to help a person react to a threat. Although stress hormones are needed at times of danger, if they remain too high for too long, the body becomes overstressed, and certain systems, such as the immune system, can't function as well. Experiments on both human infants and infant experimental animals showed these fascinating results:[40, 92, 93, 94, 184, 218]

- Human infants with the most secure attachment to their mothers had the best cortisol balance.
- The longer infant animals were separated from their mothers, the higher the cortisol levels, suggesting that these babies could be chronically stressed. The mothers also experienced elevated cortisol levels when separated from their babies.

- Prolonged cortisol elevations may diminish growth.
- Prolonged cortisol elevations may suppress the immune system.
- Infant animals separated from their mothers showed imbalances in the autonomic nervous system — the master control system of the body's physiology. They didn't show the usual increases and decreases in heart rate and body temperature, had abnormal heartbeats (called "arrhythmias"), and showed disturbances in sleep patterns, such as a decrease in REM sleep (the stage of sleep in which an infant is most arousable in response to a life-threatening event, as discussed on page 98). Similar physiological changes were measured in preschool children separated from their parents.[98]
- In addition to the agitation caused by prolonged elevation of adrenal hormones, separation sometimes caused the opposite physiological effect: withdrawn, depressed infants who had low cortisol levels.
- Separated infants showed more irregular heart rates.
- Infants separated from their mothers were less able to maintain a stable body temperature.
- Infant animals who stayed close to their mothers had higher levels of growth hormones and enzymes essential for brain and heart growth. Separation from their mothers, or lack of interaction with their mothers when they were close by, caused the levels of these growth-promoting substances to fall.[32, 128]

Clearly, the continued presence of a nurturing mother is important for the infant's physiological and emotional well-being. A secure mother-infant attachment helps an infant's physiological systems work better. Attachment organizes a baby's overall physiological systems; separation disorganizes them. And a baby with a disorganized physiology or disorganized biorhythms can be at increased risk of SIDS.[196]

Attachment researchers use the two physiological parameters

of *heart rate* and *heart-rate variability* (how well the heart changes in response to changing physiological needs) as a sort of efficiency indicator of an infant's physiological well-being. Studies show that breastfeeding newborns have lower heart rates, more heart-rate variability, improved behavioral organization, and more active sleep than bottle-feeding newborns. Also, the investigators conclude that breastfeeding newborns show a more energy-efficient behavioral organization than bottle-fed newborns do.[247] These studies suggest the physiology of a bottle-feeding baby may be like an automobile engine that is not tuned up.[91, 247]

Attachment parenting helps babies thrive. If, as we have seen, an in-arms baby cries less and is less anxious, and therefore consumes less energy, I conclude that the infant has more "free time" to divert into *thriving* energy that would otherwise have been wasted worrying and fussing. "To thrive" means more than just to grow bigger; it means to grow to one's fullest potential, physically, intellectually, and physiologically.

Attachment-parented babies feed more frequently, an interaction that itself improves growth and overall behavioral organization.[92] One of the oldest recipes for the failing-to-thrive baby is "take your baby to bed and nurse." As previously discussed, attachment promotes growth hormones and enzymes that enhance brain growth in experimental animals. Growth hormone is secreted primarily during sleep. Endocrinologists have discovered that human infants deprived of sufficient attachment have lower growth hormones and fail to thrive — a malady called "psychosocial deprivation." From these studies can we infer that attachment-parented babies have higher levels of growth-promoting hormones? Someday, I predict, research will confirm what I have long suspected: attachment-parented infants have higher levels of substances that enhance their overall physiological well-being and boost their self-protective abilities as well. So, it seems that mother, by attachment parenting, could act as a regulator of her infant's physiology, especially during the "developmental dip," the crucial two to four months when an infant is physiologically disadvantaged and at highest risk of SIDS (see page 34).

If attachment parenting puts an infant at a physiological advantage to survive the vulnerable period for SIDS, does that imply a baby who receives a more distant style of parenting is at a physiological disadvantage? I believe it does. During my twenty-five years as a pediatrician, I have cared for infants called "failure-to-thrive" babies — infants who aren't developing to their physical and psychological potential. And, often unintentionally, this condition can be due to poor quality of mother-infant attachment. For the past thirty years, pediatric textbooks have documented cases of "failure to thrive" secondary to poor attachment. Simply put, a baby who feels right, grows right; but an infant who receives less attachment than he needs in order to thrive feels psychologically unright, and this feeling translates into being physiologically unright.

Attachment parenting makes you an expert on your baby.
Besides doing good things for babies, attachment parenting helps mothers too. One of the pieces of advice I give new parents during their first well-baby visit is: "You don't have to become an expert on parenting, but you must become an expert on *your* baby, because no one else will." While it is true that many babies who die of SIDS give no warning signs that their last breath is imminent, some babies do give clues that something is not quite right. Attachment parenting can also boost your sensitivity, helping you monitor your baby appropriately. Studies have shown that improving mothering skills can lower SIDS rates. The Sheffield, England, study described on page 54 showed that high-risk families who received special parenting-skill education had a SIDS rate of 3.2 per thousand compared with 10.6 per thousand for those

THE SHUTDOWN SYNDROME — TO THE EXTREME

Could SIDS in some infants be due to an emotional disturbance that triggers the collapse of physiological control mechanisms that sustain life? While interviewing SIDS parents and reviewing SIDS research, I was intrigued by how many babies died in circumstances where there was a *change in care-giving routine:* a different bed, a new caregiver putting the baby to sleep, a different way of going to sleep. SIDS parents volunteer: "the first time I left her with a sitter"; "the first time I let him cry it out"; "the first time I put him to sleep in a crib."

Susan, whose baby died of SIDS at age four and a half months, told me, "The day Jonathan died he seemed different. He seemed distant. Yet my sister reassured me that he would be fine, so I left him in her care but told her that he was a very clingy baby and to be sure to stay with him. He died during his nap at my sister's house. That was his first time in a crib. We found him facedown with his nose in the bedding. He was so used to sleeping next to me. In my heart I believe he shut down."

Could the term "scared to death" have a biological basis? The physiological effects of attachment and separation are discussed throughout this chapter. Also, research has supported what insightful parents have long suspected: how babies feel can affect how their bodies work. Infants studied during emotional disturbances (fear, anger, pain) have shown life-threatening disturbances in their breathing and cardiovascular systems.

A "fear paralysis reflex" (similar to a cardiorespiratory arrest) has been observed in frightened animals, and this reflex is more easily triggered when the animal is in a strange environment or separated from its mother.[105]

Researchers have noted that many SIDS babies, before they died, had some environmental upsets that affected their daily or nightly rhythms. These observations support the suspicions that overall abnormalities of nervous system control may be an underlying mechanism in some SIDS infants.[151]

Throughout my years as a pediatrician, I have noticed the correlation between how well babies thrive and the degree of attachment parenting they receive. Norm and Linda were first-time parents who consulted me because their four-month-old high-need baby, Heather, had stopped growing. Heather had been a happy baby, thriving on a full dose of attachment parenting, and it was working for the family. Well-meaning friends persuaded these parents that they were spoiling their baby, that she was running their lives and manipulating them, and that she would be a clingy, dependent child forever.

Like many first-time parents, Norm and Linda lost confidence in what they were doing and yielded to the peer pressure of adopting a more restrained and distant style of parenting. Heather was left to cry herself to sleep, her feedings were scheduled, and she was not carried as much. Over the next two months Heather's weight leveled off, and she went from being happy and interactive to withdrawn. The sparkle in her eyes was gone. She was no longer thriving, and neither were her parents.

Heather was labeled by her doctor "failure to thrive" and was about to undergo an extensive medical evaluation. The parents consulted me, and I diagnosed "the shutdown syndrome" and explained that she had been thriving because of their responsive style of parenting. Her overall physiology had been organized and she had trusted that her needs would be met. In desiring to do the best for their infant, the parents had let themselves be sucked into another style of parenting. They unknowingly pulled the attachment plug on Heather; the connection that had caused her to thrive was gone. A sort of baby depression resulted, and her physiological systems slowed down. I advised the parents to return to their previous high-touch attachment–style of parenting — to carry her a lot, breastfeed her on cue, and respond sensitively to her cries by day and night. Within a month Heather was once again thriving.

A baby who shuts down becomes emotionally and physiologically disadvantaged. If this baby encounters a life-threatening situation, such as an unsafe sleeping practice (sleeping facedown on a cushioned surface), unlike the physiologically advantaged baby who would fight to breathe, this baby lacks the drive to survive and is a setup for SIDS. This physiological reaction may occur when infants are left to cry themselves to sleep. In fact, observers have noticed that many tummy-sleeping infants assume the facedown position while crying, and they postulate that such infants may stay in this position and fall asleep.[39] The relationship between how babies feel and how they thrive (or survive) is still somewhat of a mystery, and one that deserves more attention and investigation.

who received no special attention. While this extra education did not specifically mention "attachment parenting," the mothers were encouraged to breastfeed (and more did), and it seems that the closer the mothers got to their babies, the more they were able to recognize subtle signs of illness and respond intuitively with a level of care that improved their baby's well-being.

Attachment parenting is especially valuable for babies born prematurely. By breastfeeding, sleeping with her baby, and wearing her baby, mother provides a backup system for baby's immaturity. Little things mean a lot for infants at risk for SIDS Attachment parenting makes you more likely to pick up on subtle changes in your baby, and because you know so much about him, you know when and how you need to intervene. You know where and in what position baby sleeps best, how to heat baby's room, when to seek medical attention, even when to clean out his stuffy nose. You are able to spot *changes* — for the better and for the worse. The self-training of an attached mother reminds me of how the U.S. Department of Treasury trains people to spot counterfeit money. The spotters spend a long time learning what real money is like. They get a feel for real money. As a result, as soon as a counterfeit piece comes along, it triggers a "not right" alarm inside them, and they spot it.

The true story that follows occurred during the writing of this book. I was sitting at my desk one evening when my emergency beeper sounded, calling me to the hospital emergency room to evaluate a five-month-old baby who had stopped breathing. Here is the mother's story:

"We went to visit friends for dinner. We put five-month-old Alan down to sleep on an adult bed. It was a firm mattress, not soft. He had never been in an adult bed before. This was a new situation for him. As we were having dinner, I felt that he had slept a little bit too long. He was a very restless sleeper, and very sensitive to noise, and the people walking by the bedroom hadn't wakened him. A sort of alarm went off inside of me. Why isn't he waking up? An uneasy feeling shot through me, a sort of 'what's wrong with this picture?' I ran upstairs and found Alan pale, blue, not breathing, and his face down on the mattress. We couldn't remember how to do CPR. We took those classes when I was pregnant, but in the panic, you don't know how you're going to react until you pick up a baby you think is dead. (For months I had nightmares of that little blue face.) We dialed 911 and called for the paramedics as we also tried to get Alan to breathe. The paramedics seemed to be there within a couple of minutes. They just happened to be nearby. They revived Alan, and we rushed to the hospital, where we met Dr. Sears.*

"During our dinner when I had wanted to check on Alan, our friends said, 'Oh, let him sleep. You never have a break. This is your time. Why don't you just enjoy your dinner?' My insides couldn't. My instinct told me something was wrong, and I needed to listen to it rather than to what everyone else wanted. I know they wanted to have a nice dinner, especially my husband. It seemed great that Alan had been sleeping so long, but I really felt that it wasn't right. I'm glad I listened to my instinct, or I don't think Alan would be here today. (He had always been a restless sleeper, which fits the diagnosis of gastroesophageal reflux. The two previous nights were the first ones that he had ever slept through the night. We were so happy!)

"I believe one of the reasons I was so aware of Alan is that I was breastfeeding him and I held him a lot. We spent a lot of time together, and I took my cues from him instead of trying to schedule him or get him to follow my program. He never slept in bed

---

*Hospital investigation of Alan revealed gastroesophageal reflux. (See page 81 for an explanation of GER.) This condition plus, perhaps, the strange bed phenomenon (see page 26) may have triggered a prolonged apnea episode in the baby.

with me at night. I could never sleep very well with him in bed with me. (I never sleep well with my husband in bed with me either.) But we always had Alan in our room.

"This was definitely a life-changing experience for me. It was a very *confirming* experience. It taught me that I need to listen to what my instinct tells me, not to anyone else. One of the most confusing things for a first-time mother is that everyone will give her advice, and she will read books, and different doctors will tell her what she should do in different situations, especially when baby should sleep through the night, and how long he should sleep. This event made me throw away all of my 'how to get your kid to sleep through the night' books and just accept his sleep patterns as a *fact of life.* I had read all those 'let him cry it out' books, and every time I would encounter them, I couldn't do what these books said. My constitution would not allow me to let him cry or try to put him on a schedule. Alan knew when he needed to eat, I didn't.

"It's funny, because I remember that the first night we brought him home from the hospital he slept through the night. Since he was a month premature, I remember thinking 'I need to get up and wake this child up.' Yet everyone said, 'Oh, you should be so thrilled that he's sleeping through the night.' When I began waking him up and feeding him, he ended up thriving.

"What this event did is really confirm in me that I am okay as a mother, if I only listen to what's inside me and use the tools I have. I learned the importance of trusting what I believe and not what my mother-in-law told me: 'Let him sleep. Never wake a sleeping baby. And don't hold him so much, you'll spoil him. He'll get used to being held.' I felt there was something inherently wrong with that advice. A mother should want to hold her baby and be next to her baby. That's where the baby has been for nine months and that's where he wants to be.

"I learned from this experience to just parent Alan in the attachment style of parenting instead of trying to get him to fit into

FEAR OF SPOILING

"But won't all that attention spoil an infant?" you may wonder. No! Attachment parenting won't spoil your baby, and it may save your baby's life. Sometimes I feel a bit foolish even putting a label on a style of parenting that most mothers would find on their own if they were given wise advice and support from friends and family and had been parented this way themselves. Yet even though years of research and plain common sense suggest that the old spoiling theory should be placed on the back shelf in the library of bad baby advice, it is still around to influence new mothers who just want to do what's good for their baby.

If the fear of spoiling — or its modern-day cliché cousin "manipulation" — is prevalent in your parenting circle, you are hanging around with the wrong advisors. When your four-month-old crib-sleeper wakes up frequently during the night, yet settles as soon as you hold her, listen to these signals and make the needed adjustments in your nighttime parenting. Adults and young children *manipulate;* babies *communicate.*

Remember, whichever parenting style you choose, it needs to not only benefit the baby's physiology but develop your sensitivity as well. Beware, especially, of the let-baby-cry-it-out advisors who tell you to train your baby, before his time, to sleep through the night and not bother you. This detachment advice lacks scientific backup and is likely to create a distance between you and your baby, which is not only unhealthy for you and your baby, but can be downright unsafe. In order to practice attachment parenting, you may have to change your mind-set regarding the mother-infant relationship, overcome some preconceived ideas of how babies are supposed to behave, and focus on what *your baby* needs and what works best for *you.*

my life, put him on my plan, which was what most people advocated. Now, when I hold a happy, healthy toddler in my arms, I'm happy that I listened to myself."

This mother's radar system, fine-tuned over months of attachment parenting, saved her baby's life. Score a happy ending for attachment parenting.

There is a mutual giving in attachment parenting. Mother acts as a regulator of her infant's physiology, and her infant helps her develop a keen sensitivity. True, the infant is a remarkably sturdy little person, able to adjust and grow in a wide variety of parenting situations. But perhaps some infants need extra help. Could SIDS in some babies be a disease of physiological disorganization? Could attachment parenting help to counteract this disorganization by decreasing stress and providing an environment that makes up for the baby's inability to regulate himself? Could attachment parenting aid in the maturation of the respiratory control system so that an infant is able to survive threats to his breathing? These are unanswered, perhaps unanswerable, questions, yet I believe the available evidence, plus a dose of common sense, makes a good case for the idea that a mother, because of the organizing effect she has on her infant's physiology, provides protection against SIDS.

Suggesting a relationship between parenting styles and SIDS is bound to draw fire from critics who still think that parenting practices play no role in SIDS, or who do not wish to place so much emphasis on the importance of the mother-baby relationship. I wonder if modern parenting focuses on too much "stuff" and not enough on touch, and if modern baby-care practices are a trade-off of increased convenience for increased risk. It may be considered politically incorrect to speculate on this kind of life-or-death role for a mother; yet, for a few infants, it may be physiologically correct. Over the past twenty years the importance of the mother to her infant's well-being has been diluted by social and economic changes to the extent that the modern view of attachment parenting is that it is nice but not necessary. I challenge that view. As soon as we open our eyes to the time-honored fact that *mothering matters,* the better off — and perhaps safer — all babies will be. My wish is that you practice attachment parenting, not just to prevent SIDS, but because you believe it is the best for you and your baby. By receiving the gift of attachment parenting, more babies will thrive — and survive.

III

Life After SIDS

Some babies can die of SIDS even though all seven steps of this risk-reduction program are practiced. To carry on your life after losing a joyful part of it is one of the most challenging tasks you will ever face. In this part of the book, I share with you the survival tactics SIDS parents have shared with me. As you will see, the way you grieve about your infant's death will affect, for better or for worse, how you live the rest of your life. I have written this part also to help friends, family, and professionals understand the uniqueness of the grieving process and, therefore, be better equipped to support the bereaved parents as they say goodbye in a way that works for them.

Healthy Grieving

There is an old saying: "When you lose a parent, you lose your past. When you lose a spouse, you lose your present. When you lose a child, you lose your future."

LESSONS FROM THOSE WHO HAVE BEEN THERE

"Grief" is the inner anguish you feel in response to loss. "Mourning" is how you express this grief outwardly, the emotions you show and the rituals you observe to help heal the hurt.[244] Both grief and mourning help you come to terms with the reality and the finality of a loss and, eventually, get on with your life. Wearing the label "SIDS parent" must seem at times unbearable. I have never lost a child, so I cannot presume to understand this grief. Instead, in this part of the book, I am sharing with you what SIDS parents have shared with me and relying on the wisdom of grieving parents who have handled their struggle in a healthy way. Grieving is intensely personal. There are no right or wrong ways to grieve, but some ways are healthier than others. The parents with whom I talked have much to teach us about what will help and what won't. Here is what they found as they struggled to make the unbearable bearable.

Doing the impossible. Healthy grieving means finding a way to stay connected yet let go. Since you were attached to your baby, you have no choice but to grieve, and grieve deeply. It is crucial to acknowledge and let yourself feel these deep emotions in order to do the work of grieving. If you don't do this work, you will never be able to get on with your life. Doing the impossible means redefining the bond between you and your baby, not breaking it. Bonds like this don't break. You will always be connected to your baby, and she will live on in your memory and your imagination. As you gaze longingly at baby pictures, you will reflect on the beautiful baby she was. As time goes on, you will imagine the child she would have become, such as the physical features and personality she might have had, and the relationship you would have had. As you watch your other children or those of friends grow and participate in all of childhood's rituals and activities, you will be reminded of the little life that is missing, and these reminders will trigger grief that you will learn to cope with as yet another dimension of your life.

GRIEF NEEDS TO BE EXPERIENCED, NOT OVERCOME

Friends, relatives, even professionals such as clergy and doctors may not always appreciate how long the agony lasts and how deeply it runs. The myth of "getting back to normal" reflects the emotional shallowness of our quick-fix society, which is impatient and uncomfortable with people who are hurting. Employers, relatives, and friends will remind you that you have a job to do, a family to feed, and a life to live. What they are really saying is "Your grief inconveniences me, and I can't deal with it." Realize that even your closest friends may expect you to have a "stiff upper lip," to "get hold of yourself," to "show some self-control," or to "get over it." They don't understand. They've never experienced the shock of having a part of their lives ripped away without warning and without explanation. You shouldn't have to cover up your grief. Yes, time heals, but it can't erase — nor should it — the memories of someone who was once a part of you. Grieving is a long process, not an event of a few months' duration. In a sense it lasts a lifetime, though, thankfully, it doesn't hurt so deeply forever. Funerals and memorial services are healthy rituals to help soothe the intense initial pain, but the anesthetic soon wears off, and grieving continues.

WHY SIDS GRIEVING IS SO DEVASTATING

SIDS doesn't fit our accepted notions of death. It's *untimely.* Babies are supposed to grow up, not die before their parents. SIDS goes against the usual order of things. We expect elderly people to die and we can rejoice in the fruitful lives they have lived.

When a baby dies, we grieve for the life the baby should have lived. The baby was cheated out of the world's wonders, and the parents have been deprived of joys they have worked hard for and deserve. This tragedy could be termed "Sudden Parental Loss Syndrome."

If an infant or child dies of a chronic illness, we are prepared for the death. But SIDS is *unexpected* — it comes without warning, without explanation. A death from SIDS feels very wrong, and this feeling triggers and retriggers anger, making the grieving especially hard. The hardest tragedy to accept and to grieve for is one for which there is no apparent cause.

HOW YOU MAY FEEL

Grieving hurts. Because you hurt inside you may not always act "normally" on the outside. No one should expect you to. Humans are emotional beings, and troubles of the mind often trigger troubles in the body and in behavior. Here are some of the ways you may feel.

In shock. In the first hours and days after baby's death it is normal to be in a state of shock. Your mind and body are jolted and, understandably, do not work "normally." As you hold your dead baby, you may feel numb, empty, almost lifeless yourself. You may be oblivious to the sirens of the ambulances, even to the desperate attempts of the paramedics. Friends, doctors, police may ask you questions and offer advice that you don't hear, don't understand. Your life is shipwrecked and you are sinking. Your mind is a blur, your body is neutral. You can't help yourself and you don't know how to ask for help. Only the reviving of your pale, blue, still baby to a pink and perky person can revive you now, and somehow down deep you convince yourself that this is possible. You are still in a state of disbelief, denial. It really didn't happen. It couldn't have happened. It was all a dismal dream from which you hope to awaken. It all seems unreal, but this initial shock state acts as a temporary anesthetic. It actually numbs the pain.

Angry. As the shock wears off, the reality and finality of death hit. You have lost a baby — forever. "Why my baby?" "Why me?" "What happened?" "It's not right." Babies should not be snatched abruptly from life, deprived of the next seventy years. Anger is a natural and understandable reaction. You may be angry at the doctor. "You told me he was healthy yesterday. Now he's dead, and you can't tell me why!" You may be angry at the police for insensitively (and unintentionally) implying that you were a negligent parent. You may be angry at the babysitter; you may be angry at God. Most of all, you may be angry at yourself.

Guilty. The litany of "if onlys" chip away at what little glue is holding you together. "If only I hadn't put him to sleep in his own room." "If only I hadn't gone out and left him with the babysitter." "If only . . . If only . . ." It's normal to blame yourself. Part of working through tragedy is thinking that you could have controlled circumstances and thereby influenced the outcome. This fantasy somehow helps. Then you progress to the realization that bad things do happen to good people. Your baby's death was beyond your control and, therefore, you cannot blame yourself for it. Still, don't be too quick to dismiss these "if onlys"; otherwise they will crop up again and again. Ask questions of your doctor, of SIDS support group members, of your spouse. Slowly, one by one, replace each "I should have done this" with "This probably would not have saved her life." And it probably wouldn't have. Yet that "probably" will plague you forever. There will always be that nagging doubt that will feed your guilt, a remorse that time and therapy can heal but never erase. Special circumstances may intensify your guilt and thereby prolong the grieving. At a support group meeting, a SIDS mother shared, "He was fussy that day, and I was very tired. He woke up at two A.M., and I nursed him and said, 'Please sleep for a very long time because Mommy needs her rest.'" This baby never woke up.

Cheated. It is easier to cope with the death of an elder than a child. You can anticipate this death and prepare for it. The sorrow is soothed by the joyful memories of the full life lived. Not so with the SIDS infant. This baby was cheated out of a life she should have lived; the family feels cheated out of a child-adult who will never be, the ball games that will never be played, the grandchildren who will never be born.

Empty. Everywhere you look are reminders of the baby who is gone. The empty highchair, carseat, crib; the empty place at the table; the next well-baby appointment with the doctor that, along with other events, must be erased from the calendar. Time and changing circumstances will fill this void, but never completely.

Incomplete. Every time someone asks, "How many children do you have?" you are forced to bring forth the truth, awkward as it may seem initially. "Two," you answer, "Jaime, who's three, and Michael, who died." Even as you muster up an explanation (which is seldom necessary, since the person who asked wishes she hadn't and quickly changes the subject), you may feel both awkward and uncomfortable. The family portrait is now and forever incomplete.

Desiring to replace. Within an hour after her baby died, a grieving mother was pressing me to find another baby she could adopt. This initial reaction is a normal part of grieving, an overwhelming desire to have someone to fill empty arms, relieve full breasts, heal an aching heart, occupy an empty crib, bring squeals and squeaks to a quiet nursery, make a house again a home. After the shock of death wore off a bit, this mother realized her baby was not replaceable, that no live baby could overcome the memories of her dead one.

Expect friends who mean well, yet don't understand the grieving process, to offer words of "comfort" such as "You're young, you can always have more children," or "You can adopt." Statements like these devalue the intense parental connection to the lost baby, minimize the intensity of grief, and may cheapen the attachment to any future children. For healthy grieving to occur, it's important to value the connection to this baby and also to value any future baby as a special person, not as merely a replacement.

Afraid to have another baby. You may have mixed feelings about having another baby. Your heart may long for another child, but in your mind you may worry about this tragedy repeating itself. You fear you can't possibly survive the loss of another love. The desire to fill the void often overcomes the worry. The good news is that the risk of SIDS happening again in the same family is remote (see "Could It Happen Again?" page 207). New research estimates that parents have at least a 99.5 percent chance of not losing another baby to SIDS, especially if parents do their best to eliminate the risk factors that are within their control. On the other hand, professionals who help people handle grief advise parents to delay major decisions about such things as another pregnancy, a move, or a job change, until the mourning process is healthfully on its way. In fact the stresses of grieving and mourning seem to increase the chances of infertility and miscarriage when couples attempt pregnancy too soon after the loss.[148] You must outgrow your need to replace the dead child before you can look forward to another child for that individual's sake. Then having another child will fill the void in your life, giving you another person to parent rather than allowing you to imagine you are still parenting the baby who died.

Fearful and vulnerable. The shock of a great loss may leave you vulnerable to feeling "If this happened, what else may happen to me?" You may be afraid to drive for fear you might have an accident. You may be afraid to cross the street for fear you might get hit. One mother said that she panicked each time her husband didn't come home at the time he said he would. These feelings are normal (and temporary) as you grapple with and accept the reality that life has jolts that knock you down. You get up and continue on and eventually feel less fearful.

Overprotective. Another normal symptom of grieving and loss is the need to cling to treasures you still have. You may go into your three-year-old's bedroom frequently to check his breathing. It's normal to be hyperprotective after a loss. If it happened once, it could happen again. You may refuse to let your children do things you previously might have allowed. You say no to overnight camping trips with Scouts. You panic when your thirteen-year-old doesn't call at the promised time.

It's impossible not to be hypervigilant about your living children. In grieving logic, loving them is equated with the fear of losing them. While being somewhat overprotective is normal and harmless, if exaggerated, it can stifle a child's development and actually increase the risk of harm. A three-year-old who is never allowed to climb may never learn to climb safely. Realize that it's normal for you to want to protect, but that safety also depends on knowing when to let go.

Older children will understand your overprotectiveness and be willing to accept and talk it out with you. One ten-year-old caringly reminds her grieving mother, "Mom, you're being overprotective again." You might want to use humor therapeutically: "I'm about to sound overprotective, but please call me if you're going to be late." You don't always have to apologize for your worry. Children can equate a certain amount of overprotectiveness with being cared for and valued.

Forgetful. Not only do grief and loss zap your physical energy, they often drain your mind as well. You may miss freeway exits, get to the store and forget what you went for, or leave the water boiling in the kettle. You may find yourself repeating daily tasks. One mother did the same load of laundry five times before she realized it. One father had to quit driving for a while because he kept fading out and running traffic lights. Another SIDS father confessed, "I couldn't balance my checkbook, but our bank manager was very understanding." People who know about grieving will understand why you are not acting like yourself. After all, you're not yourself.

Aware of physiological changes. When the mind doesn't function well, neither does the body. When that little person who was such an important part of your life suddenly isn't there anymore, your body notices. Arms actually ache — dubbed the "empty arms syndrome." Holding something else of similar weight may soothe the feeling. Mothers, your breasts may also ache and drip with milk in the middle of the night. Other common symptoms are muscle aches, headaches, stomachaches, mood swings, daydreams, difficulty concentrating, sleep disturbances, chest pains, dizziness, and a feeling of being tied up in knots. Grieving throws the appetite out of balance — usually, but not always, in the direction of eating too little. Not paying attention to your physical needs can leave you weak, sleep-deprived, and dehydrated — in a state that lessens your ability to cope with grief.

Experiencing the ripple effect. The confusion, disorientation, and lack of energy you feel can be risky to your well-being and to your livelihood. Loss has a way of multiplying. You've lost a baby, and then grief overtakes you and prevents you from functioning. As a result, you risk losing your marriage, your job, your friendships.

Feeling a loss of identity. When you lose a baby, you lose part of yourself. The title "parent" (or "parent of a new baby"), which you labored hard for and cherished, no longer seems to have meaning. Everywhere you go you see constant reminders of what you once had and what other moms and dads still have. You may avoid playgrounds and other places where parents and children congregate. The "Mommy and Me" class once joyfully anticipated now seems incredibly foreign to you. It's hard to feel like a mommy with the "me" gone.

Experiencing hallucinations. Imagination can play tricks on grieving people. You may wake up thinking that you hear your baby crying. You may walk into the nursery expecting baby to be there. These illusions are spooky, yet they are understandable. Your baby has never really left your mind. Visions and memories are precious, and you will consciously and subconsciously cherish them.

Clinging to mementos. All around you are constant reminders of the baby who once lived in your home. Photos, toys, clothing, and furniture need to be dealt with. Some you will discard, some you will keep and treasure. It's normal to spend hours holding your baby's favorite toy. These are known as "linking objects," tangible things that help you maintain your connection to your child. If you can't hold your baby, at least you can hold her things. Friends and relatives may not understand how you can keep all those pictures and other items around. They can't comprehend; they have not had the experience of having a child die.

Having hard times. Expect ups and downs in the grieving process. Feelings come in waves and then there's a lull for a few days. Expect these peaks and valleys. Birthdays, holidays, and all the special times of the year that ring joy in most families may cause you sorrow. One six-year-old asked, "Why is Mommy always sad at Christmas?"

Special associations can replay the tragic day your baby died. One father hated rainy nights because his baby died on a rainy night. One mother fell apart each time she heard an ambulance. Another mother had a difficult time with Mother's Day: "I didn't have a baby, but I was still a mother." As you work through the grieving, and your emptiness is partially filled with some of life's many joys, these hard times will get easier, but don't expect them to disappear entirely.

Searching for answers. You may spend a lifetime searching for answers to this tragedy. "Why my baby? How could this happen?" Grief caused by SIDS is particularly unsettling because there don't seem to be answers to why your baby died. This makes acceptance particularly difficult. It's frustrating to spend hours in libraries seeking answers, only to realize that even so-called experts on SIDS don't have the information you need. Lack of cause fuels your anger: "This should not have happened. My baby was so healthy. I was such a good mother." These unanswered questions may haunt you, making grieving difficult.

Desiring to start fresh. Many SIDS parents move, change jobs, switch doctors, or make other major changes after the death of a baby. The desire to do something different may be parents' way of erasing both the guilt and the memories. They may also believe that by changing their circumstances they are lowering the risk of SIDS happening again. For some this change is therapeutic; for others it is an unhealthy escape.

The grieving process is as individual as a personality. Most parents, if allowed and supported, will experience some or all of these feelings sometime during their journey through grief and mourning. While the grieving process cannot bring your baby back to life, it can help you get on with your life.

MANAGING YOUR GRIEF

Wounds heal. Scars remain. Life goes on. To grieve in a healthy way, maintaining a healthy connection with your infant while dealing with the separation, you need to call upon many resources, both personal and professional, for help. While there is no magic formula that fits everyone, there are time-tested ways of growing while grieving that many SIDS parents and the professionals who counsel them have found useful.

Get into your grief, not out of it. After a loss, people are often urged to keep busy, to immerse themselves in their work, to have another baby quickly — to escape the grief somehow. This doesn't work, at least for SIDS grieving. Your baby will always be part of your life, and you must acknowledge this fully or the hurt will continue to fester underneath a controlled facade. Healthy grieving means getting in touch with your feelings, mourning as *you* need to mourn, and learning to live with memories that still live in your home. You will always have — and always need — a *connection* with your baby. Healthy grieving means defining how your connection with your baby will continue while at the same time you function and grow in your daily life. Avoid thinking: "I must get over this so that my life will get back to normal." Losing a baby to SIDS is now part of your normal life. The key to bereavement is coping with this fact, not escaping from it.

Get help. It is normal to want answers and support — now! If your misery needs company, join a SIDS support group. Oftentimes you can get hands-on help, or at least someone to talk to on the phone, within hours after you ask. While no one will ever know how *you* feel about *your* baby, consult the experts — other parents who have lost a baby to SIDS. They are available,

GENDER DIFFERENCES IN GRIEVING

Husbands and wives often show different mourning styles. Males are conditioned to repress their grief, females to express it. Men often intellectualize, "There's nothing I can do about it. We just have to go on with our lives." Males tend not to believe that they need help; females often immerse themselves in support groups.

Men tend to internalize their grief, immersing themselves in their work to keep busy, and employers usually reinforce this escape. Women usually get into their grief instead of trying to escape from it. When the mother is grieving deeply, the father may feel he can't afford the luxury of grieving. He may suppress his grief, certain that he has to be "the strong one" to keep the family going. However, the next week it may be the mother who holds the family together while the father struggles.

Each spouse must respect the other's way of grieving. The one who vents her feelings may accuse the feelings stuffer of not caring; the stuffer admonishes the venter, "Get hold of yourself." Acknowledge these differences in a positive way. As one husband put it, "I respect her need to go to the support group, and she respects my need to stay away." The belief that SIDS triggers divorce may be misleading. Healthy marriages survive healthy grieving; shaky ones will get even shakier. One gender may need more intimacy, the other may need less. Accusatory sparks may fly: "Leave me alone. How could you even think of having sex when our baby has died?" Be sensitive to your mate's needs. Time heals, but not quickly.

and they care. (For the support group nearest you, see "SIDS Resources," page 211.) Mourning among those who also mourn is easier and feels safer emotionally than among persons who haven't experienced this loss. Other parents in your situation will accept you and not judge whether or not you are mourning "appropriately." You can't mess up in front of them. It's okay to vent your feelings, to scream, to weep — these parents have been there too. They may be the only audience in town that willingly listens to your story over and over. Initially, you get help from your chosen group, but eventually you *give* help too. Being a support person to other parents, besides being helpful for them, is therapeutic for you.

In attending SIDS support groups, I was initially surprised at how many couples are comfortable referring to themselves as "SIDS parents." In my experience as the parent of a child with Down Syndrome, however, I learned that parents react to labels in various ways. Some have no problem being called "Down's parents." One mother told me, "I find labels offensive. I don't like being called a Down's parent or a Down's family. I am who I am, which includes this thing that has happened, but which does not define *me.*" So, if you are uncomfortable with the prevailing jargon of your chosen grief group, just omit the words that offend you.

Try to keep a balance in your support group involvement. There will be times when you need a break from answering phone calls and helping other grieving parents. It is tempting to bury yourself in a support group; sometimes you can get in over your head and wind up ignoring other aspects of your life and your family.

If after several months you still find yourself unable to get a handle on your grief, if you are unable to function in your job, your marriage, and/or are not taking care of yourself, seek professional help. The nearest SIDS Alliance affiliate may be able to recommend a professional counselor experienced in helping

grieving parents. Remember, though, that the grief of SIDS is unlike any other grief or loss. Be sure to choose a counselor who is
experienced in helping SIDS parents.

Personalize your baby. Frequently using your baby's name
keeps you connected to your infant. I have noticed that SIDS parents who use their baby's name a lot seem to deal with not being
able to carry their infants in their arms by carrying them in their
hearts. They seem to be able to come to terms with grieving in a
healthy way.

Take good physical care of yourself. Remember, grieving
depresses the mind and the body. You may not want to eat, drink,
or exercise, but you need to. Be sure to drink a lot of fluids to
keep yourself from getting dehydrated, as dehydration aggravates
depression. You may have to force yourself into an exercise routine, perhaps the ritual of a half-hour morning walk; exercise will
help your daily mood. Depression diminishes your appetite, but
you owe it to yourself to nourish your body.

Write your grief. Use your talents to handle grief. If you have
a flair for writing, compose poems if that helps. If you have mu-
sical talent, compose songs. A mother in our community writes a
quarterly column in the local SIDS newsletter in which she imag-
ines her SIDS infant growing up over the years. When I first met
this mother, I told her, "I know Michael by reading your stories."
That seemed to be a comfort to her. You may also find comfort in
the creations of others. One mother shared, "My brother wrote a
song and sang it at the service. I shall never forget that." Another
said, "My thirteen-year-old niece wrote a poem and read it at the
service." Poems are very therapeutic for the writer and the lis-
tener, especially during hard times or on special days, when grief
may be more difficult to handle. When parents read poems to and

about their baby at SIDS support groups and SIDS conferences, there is not a dry eye in the place.

HOW FRIENDS AND FAMILY CAN HELP

It's usually not what you say, but the very fact that you are there that shows you care. When it comes to helping the griever, remember that you have two ears and one mouth, which gives you a clue about whether speaking or listening is more important. Here is a poem a mother read at a SIDS conference to emphasize the importance of friends just being there and listening.

COULD YOU PLEASE JUST LISTEN?

by Debbie Gemmill

My baby has died. Please don't tell me you know how I feel. You don't. You can't. I hope you never do.

Don't tell me he's with God and I should be happy. How can I be happy when every time I go into his nursery all I see is an empty crib and toys that will never be played with? How can I be happy when my arms ache to hold him?

Please don't tell me God needed another angel. It's hard for me to understand why God would take away this little one who was so loved. Maybe I'll understand later. But for right now . . . let God find another angel.

Please, please, please don't tell me I'll have other children. Maybe I will . . . but my son was not a puppy that ran away . . . he cannot be replaced.

Maybe you could just listen when I remember out loud all the things we did together . . . the walks, the early morning feedings, the first time he rolled over. Maybe you could just sit with me while I cry over all the things we'll never do together.

Please Don't Tell Me It Could Be Worse. How?

I really don't want to hear about your grandfather's death. It's not the same. Don't think my pain will be eased by comparison. Of course I'm glad that he didn't suffer, but I'd be a lot happier if he hadn't died at all.

I know it must be hard for you, but would you mind looking at his picture just one more time? We don't have many of him, and I'm just a little bit afraid that I may forget what he looked like. He wasn't here that long, you know.

Could You Please Just Listen?

Don't tell me I'll get over it. There is no "over it," only through it. Maybe you could just be with me while I take my first steps through it.

Please don't tell me I should be glad he was just a baby, or that at least I didn't get to know him. I knew him. I knew him before I ever saw him. He is a part of me. And now he is gone. I haven't just lost a 7-month-old baby. I have lost a part of myself.

I know you mean well, but please don't expect me to tell you how to help me. I'd tell you if I knew, but right now I can hardly put one foot in front of the other. Maybe if you looked around, you could find some things to do, like taking my daughter for a walk, or doing the dishes, or making some coffee.

Please don't try to remove my pain or distract me from it. I have to feel this way now.

Maybe You Could Just Listen.

Bereaved parents are sensitive to how their friends treat them in the days after the death and for a long time thereafter. What hurts SIDS parents most is feeling abandoned. One mother said, "My closest friends didn't attend my baby's funeral. They sent me notes. I asked them why. They answered, 'We couldn't handle seeing a dead baby." I felt abandoned." Friends, if you are uneasy about comforting a friend who has lost a baby to SIDS, tell them so. Be honest and say, "I don't know what to say or do. Please help me. Tell me what you need, and I will try to do it." Don't ask "Do you need anything?" Someone who is grieving often doesn't know what he or she needs. Try to anticipate their needs; be specific: "You're probably tired of casseroles. Would you like me to bring over a salad?" When you don't know what to say, say nothing. Just be there. One mother described how her friend helped her: "I didn't remember what she said, I just remember her caring expression." Show you care, extend an invitation, make that visit. Let grieving parents know that you still want their friendship, and that their place in your heart is not contingent upon having a baby. A phone call or a note on the anniversary of baby's death lets the grieving parents know that they — and their baby — are remembered.

When help isn't help. In your zeal to rush in and help, you may unintentionally hinder the normal grieving process. A mother described this situation: "My mother-in-law, well intentioned, came into our house and removed the bottles, clothes, crib, and toys, so when I got home the nursery was empty." Dealing with the belongings of the infant is part of saying good-bye, and this has to be done at the griever's own pace.

A NOTE TO PARENTS ABOUT FRIENDS AND FAMILY

Friends will react to you in different ways. Some will rally around you and be especially tolerant and sensitive to the fact that you may not act all that "normal." Other friends are not so accepting and may distance themselves from you. Sometimes even your best friends will withdraw from you when you are grieving.

WHAT NOT TO SAY

The following are quotes SIDS parents have heard from well-meaning friends or relatives, but wish they hadn't:

- "You can always have more children."
- "You are young."
- "Having children is like playing Russian roulette."
- "At least you have other children."
- "There is always a reason."
- "It must be God's will."
- "Be glad he wasn't older. You didn't have a chance to get to know him."
- "With twins, you still have one."
- "Adopted SIDS, that must be easier — you weren't bonded."
- "God loved him more."
- "God needed him more than you did."
- "God needed another angel."
- "You must let go of your baby."
- "Tears won't bring her back."
- "Wouldn't it be better if you put away those pictures? It's been a year now since he died."
- "You have to be strong for your other children." (It is better for the children to see their parents grieve in a healthy way, to give them the message that it's okay to be sad.)
- "God only gives you so many tears, and you're going to use all of yours up."
- "He wouldn't want you to cry."
- "Men have to stay strong. How is your wife doing?"
- "At least he didn't suffer."

There are several reasons for this: First, they don't know what to do or say, so, fearful of doing the wrong thing, they do nothing. Second, your grief frightens them. They may also not want to expose their own children to the reality of your loss. This rejection is difficult to handle; you've lost your baby — you don't want to lose your friends as well. SIDS parents often report they feel excluded from activities they used to share with other families, because they no longer have a baby, and the group can't handle their grieving. Or they feel friends may worry that they will feel uncomfortable around other babies and children.

Parents, realize where your friends are coming from. It's not that they don't care; it's that they don't know what to do or say, or they have convinced themselves they simply can't handle being around your grieving. Your friends may have gotten the impression from you that you want to grieve privately, without anybody around for a while. Recognize that friends and family need to grieve too. Don't keep them away and deprive them of their chance to mourn with you.

You may need to help your friends express their feelings, and subconsciously they will welcome it: "I notice you never mention Billy's name. I need you to do this," or "It would really be helpful to me if you . . ." One friend, after hearing this, said, "Thanks for helping me. I didn't know if what I wanted to do would help or hurt." I have noticed how relatives keep connected to the baby by the titles they give themselves: "I'm a SIDS aunt," or "I'm a SIDS grandfather." Remember that staying connected to friends and family also helps you grieve in a healthy way.

Be aware of cultural differences. Some friends and family members may seem uncaring, but be aware that this may simply reflect the way they have been programmed to handle grief. A father said, "My father is Japanese and a stoical feelings stuffer. He says, 'Things just happen. . . . Get on with it now.'" Each culture has its way of handling grief. Some are very reserved; some are very emotional.

How clergy can help. All humans, including pastors, priests, and rabbis, have the ability to hurt and be hurt by others. Clergy members *do* care about grieving parents, but some have more experience than others in avoiding what's hurtful and in saying what's helpful. The following suggestions were shared with me by clergy who have dealt with grieving parents and by SIDS parents who have been helped by their clergy.

First of all, don't play God. This is not the time to sermonize, proselytize, or profess your faith. Avoid pious platitudes such as, "It's God's will," or "God has a purpose in all this." The will of God is, at times, inscrutable to humans. Remarks like this paint a picture of a malicious, capricious God rather than a loving, caring, compassionate God. Better just to convey that "God is compassionate; He will help you grieve." Offer the beatitude "Blessed are those that mourn, for they shall be comforted."

Second, allow the griever to be angry with God. Some religious counselors actually say, "If you're angry with God, be angry. God is big enough to take it. God may be the only one who truly understands." Be prepared for statements that question God's wisdom: "Why did God take my baby?" A helpful response may be to remind the griever that even Jesus questioned his own Father's will: "My God, my God, why have you forsaken me?" You may offer reassurance of a continuing connection to God, such as, "God knows better than anyone how you feel." Allow grieving parents to vent their love-hate relationship toward God: "God, I'm mad at you, but I need you." Oftentimes just your presence, and not your words, is most helpful. Many parents discover their own faith as they work through their grief.

HELPING SIBLINGS GRIEVE

Kids grieve differently from adults because kids think differently. There are ways to help your children work through their grief while you are working through yours.

Respect the uniqueness of sibling grieving. Tragedies like SIDS frighten little people. They cannot figure out why this happened, and they are less able to articulate their feelings and questions than adults are. Young minds are inquisitive, but adults often don't have the answers children want, or they are not able to present the information they have in a way that children can understand.

How children grieve depends on their stage of development. As children's cognitive skills increase, they develop a better understanding of their fears and coping mechanisms. Around six years of age a big developmental leap occurs in the ability to handle and express grief. Six-year-olds are also better able to express what's in their memory. When asked "Do you have any brothers or sisters?" the six-year-old may answer, "Yes, but he died." At three, children begin to know that death is part of life, and at six, they can begin to comprehend its permanence.

You may notice unusual conversations occurring among your children, a kind of bizarre sibling rivalry. A six-year-old and a nine-year-old were talking about their baby brother, who died of SIDS. "You never knew Michael," said the nine-year-old. (He thought this baby brother was his alone.) The six-year-old responded, "I do, too. I know him in heaven." Let children work through these dialogues as a way of working through their connection with their dead sibling. Even awkward conversations can help a child open up and express grief in a way that is comfortable for him

COULD IT HAPPEN AGAIN?

If one baby in the family dies of SIDS, are subsequent infants in this family at increased risk? Just as the term "high risk" is overused in obstetrics, a SIDS sibling may also get unfairly tagged "high risk." The issue is somewhat controversial and often produces needless worry for parents who have already lost an infant to this tragedy. "Siblings of SIDS" is an ominous label that is not usually justified. Yes, if all SIDS families were to be lumped together, the siblings of the babies who died would have a higher statistical risk of dying of SIDS. But that's because many of these risk factors are inherent in the families themselves. For example, in the National Institutes of Health Collaborative Study of eight hundred SIDS infants, 70 percent of the mothers smoked. Naturally, all the siblings of these SIDS cases will "inherit" the higher risk, not because of genetic factors, but because of the smoke in the environment. My interpretation of the studies and the statistics that go with them allows me to offer some consolation to parents who have lost a baby to SIDS and go on to have another infant. I believe that the next baby has no greater risk (or at worst, only a slightly increased risk) of dying of SIDS than any other child, provided that the following are true:

- you do not have any family environmental factors for SIDS (see list of risk factors, page 19)
- your infant who died was a typical SIDS baby, meaning that baby was in the usual age range and a cause of death was not found
- the new infant has no individual medical risk factors, such as prematurity

If there are no SIDS risk factors in your family or your baby, you need not worry about the "siblings of SIDS" risk, nor is it necessary to study or monitor your subsequent babies for signs of increased risk of SIDS. While studies show that monitoring has not statistically reduced the recurrence risk, some parents may want to have their baby electronically monitored for their own peace of mind. This request should be respected. If, however, you are a family at risk or your next baby has individual risk factors, try the SIDS prevention program outlined in this book.

What about SIDS risk in multiple births? You may hear the statistic "SIDS risk is doubled for twins and tripled for triplets." In reality, this scary statistic reflects the increase in SIDS in low birthweight infants (most multiples are premature or low birthweight). If a multiple's birthweight is greater than 2,500 grams (5½ pounds), the SIDS risk is no greater than for singleton births. Being a twin does not of itself seem to put a baby at increased risk of SIDS. Statistically, if one twin dies of SIDS, the other twin is at increased risk within the next twenty-four hours. In some cases, infection has been shown to be the cause in the deaths that occurred within twenty-four hours, and so those deaths should not be considered SIDS. The consensus is that after twenty-four hours, the risk of the other twin dying of SIDS is no greater than the average sibling rate, especially if the family practices the risk-lowering suggestions in this book.[15, 16, 37]

Use the right words. Instead of terms like "a long sleep" or "went away," use the words "death" and "died." Using figurative terms like "went to sleep" will confuse a child and make him afraid to go to sleep. Avoid messages such as "He went away for a long time" or "God called him home." Children need to believe that God is kind and caring, not a malicious being who snatches children away from their parents.

Explain death to kids on a level that they can understand. For a three- to five-year-old, death is temporary and reversible, such as going away on a long trip or being in a long sleep. From five to nine years of age, children begin to realize that death happens to people, but only to other people. After the age of nine, children begin to understand fully the finality of death and that eventually everyone dies. But no matter what the age, when they ask about death, be concrete.

Answer their questions. Our adult instinct is to protect our children from grief. But in so doing we often confuse the issue and increase their anxiety. Be honest. Kids sense when you're not being truthful. They will have questions like "Why did the baby die?" If you don't know, say so in a way that helps the child to feel more comfortable and to understand that it's okay not to know. They *will* ask, "Will it happen to me?" Children may need continued reassurance that they are not likely to die anytime soon.

Don't overdose. Just as with food, children need small, frequent feedings of information. Know when you've said enough. Children have natural defenses that protect them when the going gets tough emotionally. For example, halfway through a long explanation of how the baby died, a six-year-old may suddenly jump off her parent's lap and run outside to play, as if nothing happened. Understand that this is normal. The child is giving you the message "That's enough, that's all I can handle at this time."

Expect unusual associations. Young children make associations that may seem illogical to you but that are very logical to them. In one family, the parents were talking about going on an airplane, saying that the airplane would go up into the sky, when the five-year-old said, "Are you going to see my brother?" Another child, upon hearing they were going on a family trip asked, "Are we going to see Billy?" Young children don't think like adults. After the arrival of a new baby, one three-year-old asked, "When is Suzy going to die?" He was sure all tiny babies go on to die.

Expect sibling rivalry. A sibling may ask her mother, "Why don't you have a picture of me next to your bed?" Or, as the child notices the mother's preoccupation with mementos of the lost baby, "Why don't you hold one of my dolls?" An older child may say, "She's gone. Why don't you put her pictures away?" Much of this jealousy is due to the child's worry about what's going to happen to the family now, along with anger that the parents are so sad and preoccupied with the death. Continuing family routines as normally as possible reassures the children that family life will go on and their needs will be met. Talk to your children about their normal angry feelings over mommy and daddy being so sad all the time. Also, be sure the child feels loved for himself and not as a replacement for your SIDS baby.

Help children express their grief. Remember, not only has your job description abruptly changed, so has that of the other children. The "big brother" or "big sister" role has suddenly vanished. When a child brings up memories of the baby, share in their recollections: "You remember how you held Suzy? I remember too." Help the child crystallize the memory of the bond he or she had with the baby. The more he or she talks about doing things with the baby, the more lasting the connection.

Give the child an opportunity to unload. Some kids will stuff

SIDS RESOURCES

1. The SIDS Alliance is a national nonprofit, voluntary organization uniting individuals, families, and professionals concerned about SIDS. The Alliance and its affiliates fund medical research to discover the causes of SIDS, offer emotional support to families who have lost a baby to SIDS, and supply up-to-date information on SIDS to the general public, particularly new and expectant parents. There are currently fifty-two affiliate groups in thirty-five states. For SIDS information and the support group nearest you, contact SIDS Alliance, 1314 Bedford Avenue, Suite 210, Baltimore, MD 21208, 1-800-221-SIDS.

2. Support resources for grieving grandparents can be obtained from Alliance of Grandparents Against SIDS Tragedy (AGAST), 1415 N. Dearborn Parkway, #3A, Chicago, IL 60610, 1-312-587-3068.

3. Professional and consumer education materials can be obtained from the National SIDS Resource Center, 8201 Greensboro Drive, Suite 600, McLean, VA 22102, 1-703-821-8955.

4. Books and pamphlets on grieving and mourning can be obtained from Compassionate Friends, P.O. Box 3696, Oakbrook, IL 60522-3696, 1-708-990-0010; fax 1-708-990-0246.

or delay their own grieving to protect their parents, feeling that their parents are already too upset. Grief comes out in other ways; one child I heard about kept drawing empty beds. While artwork can be very therapeutic for children, be alert to its messages yourself. Be there to talk when your child is ready.

Get behind the eyes of your grieving child and try to see the tragedy from his or her perspective. Remember, your child is affected by two drastic changes in his life: the loss of a brother or sister and his parents' sudden transformation into people who may be sad all the time and may have little energy left for him. Try to deal with both of these issues as your child grows through his or her grieving.

Epilogue:
Where Do We Go Now?

Over the past twenty years, much progress has been made toward an understanding of SIDS. Prodded by persistent parents, lawmakers have each year allotted more money for SIDS research. The United States ranks highest in the world for money spent on SIDS research, but, while it excels in supporting SIDS organizations and grieving SIDS parents, it ranks low in its attention to SIDS prevention. Many other countries have demonstrated a 50 percent reduction in SIDS over the past five years, but the United States has shown only a slight decrease. It's time to focus on SIDS prevention. Here are some of the directions I would like to see pursued in the future:

• *Improved research: more money, better direction.* SIDS research suffers from a *translation problem.* Despite millions of dollars of government research money (more than ten million dollars spent on SIDS education and research in 1994) and thousands of SIDS studies over the past twenty years in the United States, little information has been translated into practical advice for parents. Even the phenomenally successful "Back to Sleep" program was borrowed from the British.

    The association between front-sleeping and SIDS had been suspected for nearly ten years before the U.S. Public Health

Service, in 1994, finally began disseminating this potentially life-saving information to the public. The harmful effects of smoking on infant health has been known for more than twenty years, but still there are no warning labels on cigarette advertising and packaging. SIDS is the most common cause of death in infants between one month and one year, yet the government grants less money for SIDS research and prevention than it does to subsidize the tobacco industry. If only babies could vote.

Besides lacking enough money, current SIDS research lacks direction. One of the most frustrating aspects of SIDS research is the contradictory nature of many of the studies, with one researcher claiming the methods of another were flawed. As a student of SIDS and as a taxpayer, I wonder, If the studies were flawed, why were they funded? Perhaps government funding of SIDS research should take a goal-oriented approach, a sort of management by objectives, which was so successful in the NASA program. We eventually landed a man on the moon. According to this type of approach, the unanswered questions about SIDS are proposed. Step-by-step plans are formulated to answer these questions, and multidisciplinary research teams are funded with a view toward not only answering the questions, but also translating their findings into useful information for those who pay the research bill.

- *More Healthy Start programs while baby is still in the womb.* Model programs, or at least good starts, are the Healthy Start program and the Improved Pregnancy Outcome program in Florida. One of the facts we do know about SIDS is the high correlation between how babies spend their time in the womb and their chance of later dying of SIDS. Families at highest risk for SIDS could be given intervention counseling, such as the risk-lowering benefits of attachment parenting. Women, infants, and children (WIC) programs could offer personal breastfeeding consultation and support. Some countries with a low SIDS rate, such as Japan, reinforce breastfeeding by financially supporting breastfeeding mothers.[125] Part of welfare reform could be the requirement that families take parenting classes (which would include SIDS risk-lowering factors) before being eligible for welfare. Anti-smoking campaigns for adults have been expensive and only marginally effective. This is an example of too little, too late. Instead of spending vast sums of money convincing adults to quit smoking, it would be better to spend it on convincing kids not to start and pregnant women to stop.

- ***More political pressure for SIDS prevention.***[24] SIDS organizations and a vocal group of committed SIDS parents have been largely responsible for the increase in government funding and public awareness of SIDS prevention, yet there is more that could be done. For example, I would like to see SIDS parents and SIDS organizations lobby for warning labels on cigarette packaging and advertising, and the promotion of anti-smoking programs, such as the "Kids Against SIDS" programs that are popular in other countries.

- More preventive-medicine counseling by pediatricians and family physicians. I would like to see healthcare providers offer attachment parenting advice with at least the same enthusiasm they use to promote immunizations. Why not consider breastfeeding as important as — or perhaps more important than — injectable immunizations, especially in light of the recent research showing that breastfeeding can be beneficial to reducing the risk of SIDS? Too many healthcare providers still take the nice, but not necessary approach to many of the aspects of attachment parenting. This thinking needs to change. For example, instead of discouraging parents from sleeping with their babies, which is a natural infant right, it would be better to educate parents on how to sleep with their babies more safely. SIDS is no longer the hopeless mystery it once was. There are practical steps a parent can take to reduce the worry and reduce the risk. I believe that by the year 2000 the United States will celebrate a major drop in SIDS rates. I hope this book will contribute to that goal.

References

1. Ader, R. 1969. Early experiences accelerate maturation of the twenty-four-hour adrenal cortical rhythm. *Science* 163:1225-1226.
2. American Academy of Pediatrics. 1992. AAP task force on infant position and SIDS. *Pediatrics* 89:1120-1126.
3. Anderson, C. E. S., et al. 1989. Keeping babies warm: Have we got it right? *Health Visitor* 62:372-373.
4. Anderson, E. S., et al. 1990. Factors influencing body temperature of 3-4 month infants at home during the day. *Arch. Dis. Child* 65:1308-1310.
5. Anderson, G. C. 1991. Current knowledge about skin-to-skin (kangaroo) care for preterm infants. *J. Perinatology* 11:216-226.
6. Anderson, R. B., and J. F. Rosenblith. 1971. Sudden unexpected death syndrome early indicators. *Biol. Neonat.* 18:395-406.
7. Aniansson, G., et al. 1994. A prospective cohort study on breast-feeding and otitis media in infants. *Pediatr. Infect. Dis. J.* 13:183-188.
8. Arnon, S. S. 1983. Breastfeeding and toxigenic intestinal infections: missing links in SIDS. In *Sudden infant death syndrome,* ed. J. T. Tildon et al., 539-555. New York: Academic Press.
9. Arnon, S. S., et al. 1982. Protective role of human milk against sudden death from infant botulism. *J. Pediatr.* 100:568-573.
10. Bacon, C. J., et al. 1991. How mothers keep their babies warm. *Arch. Dis. Child* 66:627-632.
11. Baker, T. L., and D. J. McGinty. 1977. Reversal of cardiopulmonary

failure during active sleep in hypoxic kittens: Implications for SIDS. *Science* 198:419-421.

12. Barr, R. G. 1986. Increased carrying reduces crying. *Pediatrics* 77:641-648.

13. Bass, M., et al. 1986. Death-scene investigation in sudden infant death. *N. Engl. J. Med.* 315:100-105.

14. Baucher, H., et al. 1988. Risk of SIDS among infants with in utero exposure to cocaine. *J. Pediatr.* 113:831.

15. Beal, S. 1989. SIDS in twins. *Pediatrics* 84:1038-1044.

16. ———. 1992. Siblings of SIDS victims. *Clinics in Perinatology* 19:839-848.

17. Beal, S., and C. Porter, 1991. SIDS related to climate. *ACTA Paediatrica Scand.* 80:278-287.

18. Beal, S. M. 1986. SIDS: epidemiological comparisons between South Australia and communities with a different incidence. *Aust. Paediatr. J.* 22 (suppl):13-16.

19. Beal, S. M., and C. F. Finch. 1991. An overview of retrospective case-control studies investigating the relationship between prone sleeping position and SIDS. *J. Paediatr. Child Health* 27:334-339.

20. Beardsmore, C. S. 1993. Clinical physiological testing and SIDS. *Acta Paediatr.* 389 (suppl):95-97.

21. Becker, L. 1990. Neural maturation delay as a link in the chain of events leading to SIDS. *Can. J. Neurol. Sci.* 17:361-371.

22. Beckerman, R. C., et al. 1992. *Respiratory control disorders in infants and children.* Baltimore: Williams and Wilkins.

23. Beckwith, J. B. 1975. The sudden infant death syndrome: A new theory. *Pediatrics* 55:583-584.

24. Bergman, A. B. 1986. *The "discovery" of sudden infant death syndrome: Lessons in the practice of political medicine.* New York: Praeger.

25. Birnbaum, D. A. 1978. Breastfeeding and the prevention of SIDS. *Medical Trial Technique Quarterly* 24:408-412.

26. Blumenthal, I., and G. T. Lealman. 1982. Effect of posture on gastroesophageal reflux in the newborn. *Arch. Dis. Child* 57:555-556.

27. Bolton, D. P. G., et al. 1993. Rebreathing expired gases from bedding: A cause of cot death? *Arch. Dis. Child* 69:187-190.

28. Bourne, A. S. 1994. Bedsharing and SIDS. *Brit. Med. J.* 308:537–538.
29. Brackbill, Y., et al. 1973. Psychophysiological effects in the neonate of the prone versus the supine placement. *J. Pediatr.* 82:82–84.
30. Burns, B., and L. Lipsitt. 1991. Behavioral factors in crib death: Toward an understanding of SIDS. *J. Appl. Dev. Psychol.* 12:159–184.
31. Butler, N. R., et al. 1972. Cigarette smoking in pregnancy: Its influence on birth weight and perinatal mortality. *Brit. Med. J.* 2:127–130.
32. Butler, S. R., et al. 1978. Maternal behavior as a regulator of polyamine biosynthesis in brain and heart of the developing rat pups. *Science* 199:445–447.
33. Caglayan, S., et al. 1991. A different approach to sleep problems of infancy: swaddling above the waist. *Turkish J. Pediatr.* 33:117–120.
34. Canet, E., et al. 1989. Effects of sleep deprivation on respiratory events during sleep in healthy infants. *J. Appl. Physiol.* 66: 1158–1163.
35. Carpenter, R. G., and J. L. Emory. 1977. Final results of study of infants at risk for sudden infant death. *Nature* 268:724.
36. Carpenter, R. G., et al. 1983. Prevention of unexpected infant death: Evaluation of the first seven years of the Sheffield intervention programme. *Lancet* 2:723–727.
37. Carroll, J. L., and G. M. Loughlin. 1993. Sudden infant death syndrome. *Pediatrics in Review* 14:83–94.
38. Chapell, M. S. 1990. SIDS (crib death) and possible relation to long-term mattress compression. *Psychological Reports* 67:1267–1272.
39. Chiodini, B. A., and B. T. Thach. 1993. Impaired ventilation in infants sleeping facedown: Potential significance for SIDS. *J. Pediatr.* 123: 686–692.
40. Coe, C. L., et al. 1985. Endocrine and immune responses to separation and maternal loss in non-human primates. In *The psychology of attachment and separation,* ed. M. Reite and T. Fields, 163–199. New York: Academic Press.
41. Coons, S., and C. Guillemmault. 1985. Motility and arousal in near-miss SIDS. *J. Pediatr.* 107:728–735.
42. Couriel, J. M., and A. Olumski. 1984. Response to acute hypercarbia in parents of victims of SIDS. *Pediatrics* 73:652–655.

43. Cunningham, A. S. 1976. Infant feeding and SIDS. *Pediatrics* 58:467-468.

44. Cunningham, A. S., et al. 1991. Breastfeeding and health in the 1980s: A global epidemiological review. *J. Pediatr.* 118:659-666.

45. Damus, K., et al. Postnatal medical and epidemiological risk factors for SIDS. In *SIDS: Risk factors and basic mechanisms,* ed. R. M. Harper and H. J. Hoffman, 187-201. New York: PMA Publishing Corp.

46. Davidson-Ward, S. L., and T. G. Keens. 1992. Prenatal substance abuse. *Clinics in P. Perinatology* 19:849-860.

47. Davies, D. P. 1985. Cot death in Hong Kong: A rare problem. *Lancet* 2:1346-1349.

48. DeJonge, G. A., et al. 1989. Cot death and prone sleeping position in the Netherlands. *BMS* 298:722.

49. Downham, M., et al. 1976. Breastfeeding protects against respiratory syncytial virus infection. *Brit. Med. J.* 2:274-276.

50. Downing, S. E., and J. C. Lee. 1975. Laryngeal chemosensitivity: A possible mechanism for sudden infant death. *Pediatrics* 55: 640-648.

51. Dwyer, T., et al. 1991. Prospective cohort study of prone sleeping and SIDS. *Lancet* 337:1244-1247.

52. ———. 1995. The contribution of changes in the prevalance of prone sleeping position to the decline in SIDS in Tasmania. *JAMA* 273:783-789.

53. Elias, M. F. 1986. Sleep-wake patterns of breastfed infants in the first two years of life. *Pediatrics* 77:322-329.

54. Emde, R. N., and R. J. Harmon. 1982. *The development of attachment and affiliative disorders.* New York: Plenum Press.

55. Emery, J. L. 1993. The dangers of soft bedding for infants. *Arch. Dis. Child* 69:711.

56. Emery, J. L., and J. A. Thornton. 1968. Effects of obstruction to respiration in infants, with particular reference to mattresses, pillows and their coverings. *Brit. Med. J.* 3:209-213.

57. Engelberts, A. C., and G. A. DeJonge. 1990. Choice of sleeping position for infants: Possible association with cot death. *Arch. Dis. Child* 65: 462-467.

58. Faroogi, I. 1994. Bedsharing and smoking in SIDS. *Brit. Med. J.* 308:204- 205.

59. Finlay, F. O., and P. T. Rudd. 1993. Current concepts of the aetiology of SIDS. *Br. J. Hosp. Med.* 49:727-731.

60. Fleming, P. J. 1994. Proceedings of the fourth annual SIDS alliance national conference, Orlando, November 9-12.

61. ———. 1994. Understanding SIDS Risk: The Avon population-based studies of epidemiology and physiology. Paper presented at the 12th Apnea of Infancy Conference, Rancho Mirage, California.

62. Fleming, P. J., et al. 1982. Changes in respiratory pattern resulting from the use of a face mask to record respiration in newborn infants. *Pediatr. Res.* 16:1031-1034.

63. ———. 1992. Development of thermoregulation in infancy: Possible implications for SIDS. *J. Clin. Pathol.* 45 (suppl.):17-19.

64. ———. 1994. Thermal balance and metabolic rate during upper respiratory tract infection in infants. *Arch. Dis. Child* 70: 187-191.

65. ———. 1994. The effects of thermal care, maternal smoking and breastfeeding on respiratory illness in infants. *Pediatr. Pulmonol.* 18:391.

66. Franco, P., et al. 1994. Decreased response to auditory stimulation in healthy infants. *Pediatr. Pulmonol.* 18:391.

67. Freed, G. E., et al. 1994. SIDS prevention and an understanding of selected clinical issues. *Ped. Clin. N.A.* 41:967-990.

68. Gidding, S. S., and M. Schydlower. 1994. Active and passive tobacco exposure: A serious pediatric health problem. *Pediatrics* 94:750-751.

69. Gilbert, R., et al. 1992. Combined effect of infection and heavy wrapping on the risk of SIDS. *Arch. Dis. Child* 67:171-177.

70. Gilbert-Barness, E., et al. 1991. Hazards of mattresses, beds and bedding in deaths of infants. *Am. J. Forensic Med. Path.* 12:27-32.

71. Gilles, F. H., et al. 1979. Infantile alantooccipital instability: The potential danger of extreme extension. *Am. J. Dis. Child* 133:30-37.

72. Glomb, W. B., et al. 1992. Hyperapnic and hypoxic ventilatory responses in school-aged siblings of SIDS victims. *J. Pediatr.* 121:391-398.

73. Goodman, A., et al. 1990. *The pharmacologic basis of therapeutics.* New York: Pergamon Press.

74. Goyco, P. G., and R. C. Beckerman. 1990. Sudden infant death syndrome. *Current Problems in Pediatrics* June:299–346.

75. Gozal, D., et al. 1988. Environmental overheating as a cause of transient respiratory chemoreceptor dysfunction in an infant. *Pediatrics* 82: 738–740.

76. Graf, M. V., et al. 1984. Presence of delta sleep-inducing peptide-like material in human milk. *J. Clin. Endocrinol. Metab.* 59:127.

77. Grether, J., et al. 1990. SIDS among Asians in California. *J. Pediatr.* 116: 525–528.

78. Griffin, M. R., et al. 1988. SIDS after immunization with the DPT vaccine. *N. Engl. J. Med.* 319:618.

79. Groswasser, J., et al. 1994. Bodyrocking decreases the number of obstructive events in infants. *Pediatric Pulmonol.* 18:392–393.

80. Grover, G., et al. 1994. The effects of bundling on infant temperature. *Pediatrics* 94:669–673.

81. Guillemmault, C., et al. 1981. Sleep parameters and respiratory variables in near-miss SIDS infants. *Pediatrics* 68:354.

82. Guntheroth, W. G. 1989. *Crib death: The sudden infant death syndrome.* New York: Futura.

83. Guntheroth, W. G., and P. S. Spiers. 1992. Sleeping prone and the risk of SIDS. *JAMA* 267:2359–2362.

84. Haddad, G., et al. 1981. Abnormal maturation of sleep states in infants with aborted SIDS. *Pediatr. Rev.* 15:1055.

85. Haglund, B. 1993. Cigarette smoking and SIDS: Some salient points in the debate. *Acta Paediatr. Suppl.* 389:37–39.

86. Haglund, B., and S. Cnattingius. 1990. Cigarette smoking as a risk factor for SIDS: A population-based study. *Am. J. Public Health* 80:29–32.

87. Harper, R. M., et al. 1981. Periodicity of sleep states is altered in infants at risk for SIDS. *Science* 213:1030–1032.

88. ———. 1982. Developmental patterns of heart rate and heart rate variability during sleep and waking in normal infants and infants at risk for SIDS. *Sleep* 5:28–38.

89. Heacock, H. J., et al. 1992. Influence of breast versus formula milk

on physiological gastroesophageal reflux in healthy newborn infants. *J. Pediat. Gastroenterol. Nutr.* 14:41–46.

90. Hendershot, G. E. 1984. Trends in breastfeeding. *Pediatrics* 74:591–602.

91. Hienig, M., et al. 1993. Energy and protein intakes of breast-fed and formula-fed infants during the first year of life and their association with growth velocity (the Darling Study). *Am. J. Clin. Nutr.* 58:152–161.

92. Hofer, M. 1982. Some thoughts on "the transduction of experience" from a developmental perspective. *Psychosom. Med.* 44:19.

93. ———. 1983 The mother-infant interaction as a regulator of infant physiology and behavior. In *Symbiosis in parent-offspring interactions,* ed. Rosenblum and Moltz. New York: Plenum.

94. Hofer, M., and H. Shair. 1982. Control of sleep-wake states in the infant rat by features of the mother-infant relationship. *Devel. Psychobiol.* 15:229–243.

95. Hoffman, H., et al. 1988. Risk for SIDS: Results of NICHD SIDS cooperative epidemiological study. *Ann. N.Y. Acad. Sci.* 533:13–30.

96. Hoffman, H. J. 1987. DPT immunization and SIDS. *Pediatrics* 79:598–611.

97. Hoffman, H. J., and L. S. Hillman. 1992. Epidemiology of SIDS: maternal, neonatal and postneonatal risk factors. *Clinics in Perinatology* 19:717–737.

98. Hollenbeck, A. R., et al. 1980. Children with serious illness: behavioral correlates of separation and solution. *Child Psychiatry and Human Development* 11:3–11.

99. Hoppenbrouwers, T., and J. E. Hodgman. 1982. SIDS: An integration of ontogenetic pathologic, physiologic and epidemiologic factors. *Neuropediatrics* 13:36–51.

100. Hoppenbrouwers, T., et al. 1982. Body movements during quiet sleep (QS) in subsequent siblings of SIDS. *Clinical Research*: 30, 136a.

101. Huang, S. 1983. Infectious diseses, immunology and SIDS: An overview. In *Sudden infant death syndrome,* ed. J. T. Tildon, et al., 593–606. New York: Academic Press.

102. Hunt, C. E. 1992. The cardiorespiratory control hypothesis for SIDS. *Clinics in Perinatology* 19:757-771.

103. ———. Sudden infant death syndrome. In *Respiratory control disorders of infants and children,* ed. R. C. Beckerman et al. Baltimore: Williams and Wilkins.

104. Jones, M. F., et al. 1994. The relation between climatic temperature and SIDS differs among communities: Results from an ecologic analysis. *Epidemiology* 5:332-336.

105. Kaada, B. 1991. An emotional trigger mechanism for sudden infant death. *Arch. Dis. Child* 66:274.

106. Kahn, A., and D. Blum. 1982. Phenothiazines and SIDS. *Pediatrics* 70:78.

107. Kahn, A., et al. 1993. Prone or supine position and sleep characteristics in infants. *Pediatrics* 91:1112-1115.

108. Keens, T., et al. 1990. Risk of SIDS in ISAM. *J. Pediatr.* 876.

109. Keens, T. G., and A. L. Vanderhol. 1984. Use of hypoxic and hypercarbic arousal responses in evaluation of infant apnea. *Perinatol. Neonatol.* 8:32.

110. Keitel, H. G., et al. 1960. Diaper rash, self-inflicted excoriations, and crying in full-term newborn infants kept in the prone or supine position. *J. Pediatr.* 57:884-886.

111. Kelly, D. H. 1994. Proceedings of the fourth annual SIDS alliance national conference, Orlando, November 9-12.

112. Kelly, D. H., et al. 1991. Sudden severe brachycardia in infancy. *Pediatr. Pulmonol.* 10:199-204.

113. Kemp, J. S., and B. T. Thach. Sudden death in infants sleeping on polystyrene-filled cushions. *N. Engl. J. Med.* 324:1858-1864.

114. Kerslake, D. M. 1991. The insulation provided by infants' bed clothes. *Ergonomics* 34:893-907.

115. Kinmouth, A. L. 1990. Review of the epidemiology of SIDS and its relationship to temperature regulation. *Brit. J. Gen. Practice* 40:161-163.

116. Kinney, H. C., et al. 1983. Reactive gliosis in the medulla oblongata of victims of SIDS. *Pediatrics* 72:181-187.

117. ———. 1991. Delayed central nervous system myelination in SIDS. *J. Neuropathol. Exp. Neurol.* 50:29-48.

118. ———. 1992. The neuropathology of SIDS: A review. *J. Neuropathol. Exp. Neurol.* 51:115-126.

119. ———. 1993. Early developmental changes in (3H) nicotine binding in the human brainstem. *Neuroscience* 55(4):1127-1138.

120. Kleinman, R. E., and W. A. Walker. 1979. The enteromammary immune system: An important new concept in breast milk host defense. *Dig. Dis. Sci.* 24:876.

121. Klonoff-Cohen, H. S., et al. 1995. The effect of passive smoking and tobacco exposure through breast milk on SIDS. *JAMA* 273: 795-798.

122. Konner, M. J. 1981. Evolution of human behavior development. In *Handbook of cross-cultural human development*, ed. R. Monroe and B. Whiting, 3-52. New York: Garland.

123. Korner, A. F., and E. Thoman. 1970. Visual alertness in neonates as evoked by maternal care. *J. Exp. Child Psychol.* 10:67.

124. Korner, A. F., et al. 1983. Effects of vestibular-proprioceptive stimulation on the neurobehavioral development of preterm infants: A pilot study. *Neuropediatrics* 14:170-175.

125. Korte, D. 1992. Infant mortality: Lessons from Japan. *Mothering* Winter:83-89.

126. Krous, H. F. 1995. Autopsy findings in SIDS victims. Proceedings of the 13th Apnea of Infancy Conference, Rancho Mirage, California.

127. Krous, H. F., and J. Jordan. 1984. A necropsy study of distribution of petechiae in non-sudden infant death syndrome. *Arch. Pathol. Lab. Med.* 108:75-76.

128. Kuhn, C. M., et al. 1978. Selective depression of serum growth hormone during maternal deprivation in rat pups. *Science* 201:1035-1036.

129. Lebrecque, M., et al. 1993. Feeding and urine cotinine values in babies whose mothers smoke. *Pediatrics* 83:93-97.

130. Lehtovirta, P., and M. Forss. 1978. The acute effect of smoking on the intervillous blood flow of the placenta. *Br. J. Obstet. Gynaecol.* 85:729.

131. Leistner, H. L., et al. 1980. Heart rate and heart rate variability during sleep in aborted SIDS. *J. Pediatr.* 97:51-55.

132. Leventhal, J. M., et al. 1986. Does breastfeeding protect against in-

fections in infants less than three months of age? *Pediatrics* 78:896–903.

133. Lewis, K. W., and E. M. Bosque. 1994. Deficient hypoxia arousal response in infants of smoking mothers. *Pediatr. Pulmonol.* 18:393–394.

134. Lewis, N. C. 1988. Ventilatory chemosensitivity in parents of infants with SIDS. *J. Pediatr.* 113:307–311.

135. Lozoff, B., and G. Brittleham. 1979. Infant care: Cache or carrying? *J. Pediatr.* 95:478–483.

136. Lucas, A., et al. 1992. Breast milk and subsequent intelligence quotient in children born preterm. *Lancet* 339:261–264.

137. ———. 1994. A randomized multicentre study of human milk versus formula and later development in perterm infants. *Arch. Dis. Child* 70:141–146.

138. Ludington-Hoe, S. M. 1993. *Kangaroo care.* New York: Bantam.

139. Luke, J. L. 1978. Sleeping arrangements of SIDS victims in the District of Columbia: A preliminary report. *J. Forensic Sci.* 23:397.

140. Luke, J. L., et al. 1974. Bed-sharing deaths among victims of SIDS: A riddle within a conundrum. *Forensic Sci. Gaz.* 5:3–4.

141. Lukkainen, P., et al. 1994. Changes in fatty acid composition of preterm and term human milk from one week to six months of lactation. *J. Ped. Gastro. Nutr.* 18:355–360.

142. Lumley, J., and J. Astbury. 1991. Advice in pregnancy. In *Effective care in pregnancy and childbirth,* ed. I. Chalmers et al., 242–247. New York: Oxford.

143. Lyon, A. J. 1983. Effects of smoking on breastfeeding. *Arch. Dis. Child* 58:378–380.

144. MacFadyen, U. M., et al. 1983. Gastro-esophageal reflux in near-miss SIDS or suspected recurrent aspiration. *Arch. Dis. Child* 58:87–91.

145. Makrides, M., et al. 1994. Fatty acid composition of brain, retina and erythrocytes in breast and formula-fed infants. *Am. J. Clin. Nutr.* 60:189–194.

146. Malloy, M. H., et al. 1988. The association of maternal smoking with age and cause of infants deaths. *Am. J. Epidemiology* 128:46–55.

147. ———. 1992. SIDS and maternal smoking. *Am. J. Public Health* 82: 1380-1382.

148. Mandell, F., and L. Wolfe. 1985. SIDS and subsequent pregnancies. *Pediatrics* 56:774-776.

149. Martin, R. J., et al. 1979. Effect of supine and prone positions on arterial oxygen tension in the preterm infant. *Pediatrics* 63:528-553.

150. Martin, T. R., and M. B. Bracken. 1986. Association of low birth weight with passive smoke exposure in pregnancy. *Am. J. Epidemiology* 124:633-642.

151. Matthews, T. G. 1992. The autonomic nervous sytsem — a role in SIDS. *Arch. Dis. Child* 67:654-656.

152. McCulloch, K., et al. 1982. Arousal responses in near-miss SIDS and in normal infants. *J. Pediatr.* 101:911.

153. McKenna, J. J., et al. 1993. Infant-parent co-sleeping in an evolutionary perspective: Implications for understanding infant sleep development and SIDS. *Sleep* 16:263-282.

154. Meyer, M. B., and G. W. Comstock. 1972. Maternal cigarette smoking and perinatal mortality. *Am. J. Epidemiology* 96:1-3.

155. Meyers, W. F., and J. J. Herbst. 1982. Effectiveness of positioning therapy for gastroesophageal reflux. *Pediatrics* 69:768-772.

156. Milerad, J., and J. Rajs. 1991. Nicotine metabolites in the pericardial fluid in SIDS. *Pediatr. Res.* 29:93.

157. Milerad, J., and H. Sundell. 1993.Nicotine exposure and the risk of SIDS. *Acta Paediatr. Suppl.* 389:70-72.

158. Mitchell, E. A. 1991. Sleeping position and cot deaths. *Lancet* 338:192.

159. Mitchell, E. A., and R. Scragg. 1993. Are infants sharing a bed with another person at increased risk of SIDS? *Sleep* 16:387-389.

160. Mitchell, E. A., et al. 1991. Results of the first year of the New Zealand cot death study. *N.Z. Med. J.* 104:72-76.

161. Morrow-Tlucak, M., et al. 1988. Breastfeeding and cognitive development in the first two years of life. *Soc. Sci. Med.* 26:635-639.

162. Mosko, S., et al. 1994. Infant sleeping position and CO_2 environment during co-sleeping: The parents' contribution. *Pediatr. Pulmonol.* 18: 394.

163. Moskowitz, W. B., et al. 1990. Lipoprotein and oxygen transport al-

terations in passive smoking pre-adolescent children. *Circulation* 586-592.

164. Naeye, R. L. 1973. Pulmonary artery abnormalities in SIDS. *N. Engl. J. Med.* 289:1167-1170.

165. ———. 1980. Sudden infant death. *Sci. Am.* 242:56-62.

166. Naeye, R. L., and E. C. Peters. 1984. Mental development of children whose mothers smoked during pregnancy. *Obstet. Gynecol.* 64:601-607.

167. Naeye, R. L., et al. 1976. Brainstem and adrenal abnormalities in SIDS. *Am. J. Clin. Pathol.* 66:526-530.

168. ———. 1976. Carotid body in SIDS. *Science* 191:567-569.

169. Navelet, Y., et al. 1984. Nocturnal sleep organization in infants "at risk" for SIDS. *Pediatr. Res.* 18:654-657.

170. Nelson, E. A. S., et al. 1989. Sleeping position and infant bedding may predispose to hyperthermia and the sudden infant death syndrome. *Lancet* (January 28th):199-200.

171. Newman, N. M., et al. 1983. Infant death and sheepskin rugs. *Med. J. of Australia* (May 14):453.

172. Nyboe, A., et al. 1982. Suppressed prolactin but normal neurophysin levels in cigarette smoking breastfeeding women. *Clin. Endocrin.* 17:363-368.

173. Orenstein, S. R. 1988. Effect of non-nutritive sucking on infant GER. *Pediatric Res.* 24:38-40.

174. ———. 1994. The prone alternative. *Pediatrics* 94:104-105.

175. Orenstein, S. R., and P. F. Whitington. 1983. Positioning for prevention of gastroesophageal reflux. *J. Pediatr.* 103:534-537.

176. Orr, W. C. 1980. Arousal from sleep: Is a good night's sleep really good? *Intern. J. Neuroscience* 11:143-144.

177. *Pediatric News.* Gravida's smoking, drug abuse suspected to play a role in SIDS. February 1991.

178. Philipp, K., et al. 1984. Effects of smoking on uteroplacental blood flow. *Gynecol. Obstet. Invest.* 17:179-821.

179. Ponsonby, A. L., et al. 1992. Characteristics of the infant thermal environment in the control population of a case control study of SIDS. *J. Pediatr. and Child Health* 1:S36-40.

180. ———. 1992. Thermal environment and SIDS: Case control study. *Br. Med. J.* 304:277–282.

181. ———. 1993. Factors potentiating the risk of SIDS associated with the prone position. *N. Engl. J. Med.* 329:377–382.

182. Poswillo, D., and E. Alberman, ed. 1992. *Effects of smoking on the fetus, neonate, and child.* New York: Oxford.

    a. Baird, D. D. Evidence for reduced fecundity in female smokers, 5–22.

    b. Campbell, O. Ectopic pregnancy and smoking: Confounding or causality, 23–44.

    c. Evans, J., and J. Golding. Parental smoking and respiratory problems in childhood, 121–137.

    d. Hall, M. H., and V. Harper. Smoking and pre-eclampsia, 81–88.

    e. MacArthur, C., and G. Fox. Prevention of smoking in pregnancy: Results of intervention, 171–180.

    f. Nicholl, J., and A. O'Cathain. Antenatal smoking, postnatal passive smoking, and SIDS, 141.

    g. Pollack, J. I. A preliminary analysis of interactions between smoking and infant feeding, 108–120.

    h. Rush, D. Exposure to passive cigarette smoking and child development: An updated critical review, 150–170.

    i. Seller, M. J., et al. Effects of maternal tobacco smoke inhalation on early embryonic growth, 45–59.

    j. Symonds, E. The effect of smoking on oxygen transfer and placental circulation, 73–80.

183. Rawson, D., et al. 1988. Rectal temperature of normal babies the night after first DPT immunization. *Arch. Dis. Child* 65:1305–1307.

184. Reite, M., and J. P. Capitanio. 1985. On the nature of social separation and social attachment. In *The Psychobiology of Attachment and Separation,* ed. M. Reite and T. Fields, 228–238. New York: Academic Press.

185. Richter, C. P. 1957. On the phenomenon of sudden death in animals and man. *Psychosom. Med.* 19:191–198.

186. Roffwarg, A. P., et al. 1966. Ontogenetic development of the human sleep-dream cycle. *Science* 152:604–619.

230 - REFERENCES

187. Saigal, S., et al. 1986. Randomized clinical trial of an oscillating air mattress in preterm infants: Effects on apnea, growth, and development. *J. Pediatr.* 109:857–864.

188. ———. 1992. Sleep state organization in normal infants and victims of the sudden infant death syndrome. *Pediatrics* 89:865–870.

189. Schechtman, V. L. 1988. Cardiac and respiratory patterns in normal infants and victims of SIDS. *Sleep* 11:413–424.

190. ———. 1989. Heart rate variation in normal infants and victims of SIDS. *Early Hum. Dev.* 19:167–181.

191. Scher, M. S., et al. 1992. Maturational aspects of sleep from birth through early childhood. In *Respiratory control disorders in infants and children,* ed. R. Beckerman et al., 89–90. Baltimore: Williams and Wilkins.

192. Schoendorf, K. C., and J. L. Kiely. 1992. Relationship of SIDS to maternal smoking during and after pregnancy. *Pediatrics* 90:905–908.

193. Scragg, R., et al. 1993. Bedsharing, smoking and alcohol in SIDS. *Brit. Med. J.* 307:1312–1318.

193a. Sears, W. 1985. *The fussy baby,* 63. New York: La Leche.

194. ———. 1985. Nighttime parenting and sudden infant death syndrome. In *Nighttime parenting — how to get your baby and child to sleep.* New York: La Leche.

195. ———. 1985. The protective effects of sharing sleep. Can it prevent SIDS? Paper presented at the International Congress of Pediatrics, Honolulu.

196. ———. 1988. *Growing together: A parent's guide to baby's first year,* 12–13. Schaumburg, Ill.: La Leche.

197. Sears, W., and M. Sears. 1993. *The baby book.* Boston: Little, Brown.

198. ———. 1994. *The birth book.* Boston: Little, Brown.

199. Sears, W., et al. 1993. The effect of co-sleeping on infant breathing — implications for SIDS. Paper presented at the 11th Apnea of Infancy Conference, Rancho Mirage, California.

200. Sexton, M., and J. R. Hebel. 1984. A clinical trial of changes in maternal smoking and its effect on birthweight. *JAMA* 251:911–915.

201. Shannon, D. C., et al. 1977. Abnormal regulation of ventilation in infants at risk for SIDS. *N. Engl. J. Med.* 297:747-750.

202. Sheldon, J. H., et al. 1992. Normal sleep in children and young adults. In *Pediatric sleep medicine,* ed. S. H. Sheldon et al. Philadelphia: W. B. Saunders.

203. Siebert, J. R., and J. E. Haas. 1988. The size of the tongue in SIDS. In *The sudden infant death syndrome: Cardiac and respiratory mechanisms and interventions,* ed. P. J. Schwartz et al., 467. Annals of the New York Academy of Sciences:533.

204. Southall, D. P., et al. 1983. Indentification of infants destined to die unexpectedly during infancy. *Br. Med. J.* 286:1092-1096.

205. ———. 1990. Recurrent cyanotic episodes with severe arterial hypoxaemia and intrapulmonary shunting: A mechanism for sudden death. *Arch. Dis. Child* 65:953-961.

206. Spiers, P. S., and W. G. Guntheroth. 1994. Recommendations to avoid the prone sleeping position and recent statistics for SIDS in the United States. *Arch. Pediatr. Adolesc. Med.* 148:141-146.

207. Spitzer, A. R., and E. Gibson. 1992. Home monitoring. *Clin. in Perinat.* 19:907-926.

208. Spoelstra, A. J., et al. 1973. Dynamic pressure-volume relationship of the lung and position in the healthy neonate. *Acta Paediatr. Scand.* 62:176-180.

209. Stanton, A. N. 1983. SIDS and phenothiazines. *Pediatrics* 71:986-987.

210. Sterman, M. B., and J. Hodgman. 1988. The role of sleep and arousal in SIDS. In *Sudden infant death syndrome: Cardiac and respiratory mechanisms and intervention,* ed. P. J. Schwartz et al., 48-62. Annals of the New York Academy of Sciences: 533.

211. Stewart, M. W., and L. A. Stewart. 1991. Modification of sleep respiratory patterns by auditory stimulation: Indications of a technique for preventing SIDS. *Sleep* 14:241-248.

212. Sunderland, R., and J. L. Emery. 1981. Febrile convulsions and cot deaths. *Lancet* 2:176-180.

213. Swift, P. F. G., and J. L. Emery. 1973. Clinical observations on response to nasal occlusion in infancy. *Arch. Dis. Child* 48:947.

214. Takeda, K. 1987. A possible mechanism of SIDS. *J. Kyoto Pref. Univ. Med.* 96:965-968.

215. Tasaki, H. M., et al. 1988. The incidence of SIDS in Saga prefecture (1981-1985). *J. Pediatr. Assn. of Japan* 92:364-368.

216. Taylor, B. J., et al. 1991. A review of epidemiological studies of SIDS in southern New Zealand. *J. Pediatr. Child Health* 27:344-348.

217. Temboury, M. C., et al. 1994. Influence of breastfeeding on the infant's intellectual development. *J. Ped. Gastro. Nutr.* 18:32-36.

218. Tennes, K. 1982. The role of hormones in mother-infant transactions. In *The development of attachment and affiliative systems,* ed. R. N. Emde and R. J. Harmon, 75-80. New York: Plenum.

219. Thach, B. T., et al. 1992. Control of breathing during asphyxia and autoresuscitation. Paper presented at the 10th Apnea of Infancy Conference, Rancho Mirage, California.

220. Thoman, E. B., and S. E. Gramm. 1986. Self-regulation of stimulation by premature infants. *Pediatrics* 78:855-860.

221. Tonkin, S. 1975. Sudden infant death syndrome: A hypothesis of causation. *Pediatrics* 55:650-661.

222. ———. 1988. The breast bottle. In *Sudden infant death syndrome: Risk factors and basic mechanisms,* ed. H. J. Hoffman. New York: PMA.

223. Tonkin, S., et al. 1979. The pharyngeal effect of partial nasal obstruction. *Pediatrics* 63:261-271.

224. Valdes-Dapena, M. 1988. A pathologist's prospective on possible mechanisms in SIDS. In *Sudden infant death syndrome: Cardiac and respiratory mechanisms and interventions,* ed. P. J. Schwartz et al., 31-36. Annals of the New York Academy of Sciences: 533.

225. Valimaki, I. A. T., et al. 1988. Heart-rate variability and SIDS. In *Sudden infant death syndrome: Cardiac and respiratory mechanisms and interventions,* ed. P. J. Schwartz et al., 228-237. Annals of the New York Academy of Sciences: 533.

226. Vandenplas, Y., and L. Sacre. 1985. Seventeen-hour continuous esophageal pH monitoring in the newborn: Evaluation of the influence of position in asymptomatic and symptomatic babies. *J. Pediatr. Gastroenterol. Nutr.* 4:356-361.

227. Vanderhol, A. L., et al. 1985. Hypoxic and hyperapnic arousal re-

sponses and prediction of subsequent apnea in infancy. *Pediatrics* 75:848–854.

228. Vertes, R. P., and G. W. Perry. 1992. Sudden infant death syndrome: A theory. *Neurosci. and Behav. Rev.* 17:305–312.

229. Wagaman, M. J., et al. 1979. Improved oxygenation and lung compliance with prone positioning of neonates. *J. Pediatr.* 94:787–791.

230. Wailoo, M. P., et al. 1990. Disturbed nights and 3–4 month infants: The effects of feeding and thermal environment. *Arch. Dis. Child* 65:499–501.

231. Walterspiel, J. N., et al. 1994. Secretory anti-Giardia Lamblia antibodies in human milk: Protective effect against diarrhea. *Pediatrics* 93:28–31.

232. Ward, S. L. D., et al. 1990. SIDS in infants of substance-abusing mothers. *J. Pediatr.* 117:876.

233. ———. 1992. Hypoxic arousal responses in normal infants. *Pediatrics* 89:860–864.

234. Watkins, C. G., and G. L. Strope. 1986. Chronic carbon monoxide poisoning as a major contributing factor in SIDS. *Am. J. Dis. Child* 140:619.

235. Weissbluth, M., et al. 1982. Sleep apnea, sleep duration and infant temperament. *J. Pediatrics* 101:307–310.

236. Widdicomb, J. G. 1981. Nervous receptors in the respiratory tract and lungs. In *Regulation of breathing,* ed. T. F. Horbein, 1:433. New York: Mariel Dekker.

237. Wigfield, R. E. 1993. How much wrapping do babies need at night? *Arch. Dis. Child* 69:181–186.

238. Wigfield, R. E., et al. 1992. Can the fall in Avon's sudden infant death rate be explained by the observed sleeping position changes? *Brit. Med. J.* 304:282–283.

239. Williams, A. 1979. Increased muscularity of the pulmonary circulation in victims of SIDS. *Pediatrics* 63:18–24.

240. Williams, A. L., et al. 1984. Respiratory viruses and SIDS. *Brit. Med. J.* 288:1491–1493.

241. Williams, S. M. 1990. Growth velocity before SIDS. *Arch. Dis. Child* 65:1315–1318.

242. Willinger, M., et al. 1991. Defining SIDS: Deliberations of an expert

panel convened by the National Institute of Child Health and Human Development. *Pediatr. Pulmonol.* 11:677–684.

242a. ———. 1994. Infant sleep position and risk for SIDS. *Pediatrics* 93:814–819.

243. Wilson, S. L., et al. 1980. Upper airway patency in the human infant: Influence of airway pressure and posture. *J. Appl. Physiol.* 48:500–504.

244. Wolfelt, A. D. 1987. Understanding common patterns of avoiding grief. *Thanatos* Summer:2–5.

245. Woo, M. S., et al. 1991. Heart variability in infants at increased risk for SIDS. *Pediatr. Pulmonol.* 11:378.

246. Wooley, P. V. 1945. Mechanical suffocation during infancy: Relation to total problem of sudden death. *Pediatrics* 26:572–575.

247. Zeskind, P. S., et al. 1992. Rhythmic organization of heart rate in breast-fed and bottle-fed newborn infants. *Early Development and Parenting* 1:79–87.

Index